Yearnings for Peace:

Assemble the Worldwide Orchestra

Yearnings for Peace:

Assemble the Worldwide Orchestra

Edited by Darlene A. Caswell

Adult Ministries
Reorganized Church of Jesus Christ of Latter Day Saints
Herald Publishing House
Independence, Missouri

Table of Contents

Introduction: *Darlene A. Caswell* 7

Chapter 1: Assemble the Orchestra
Howard S. Sheehy Jr. 11

Chapter 2: Australia: How Do Australians Value Peace?
Rick Sarre 17

Chapter 3: French Polynesia: Hau, Aroha, Peace
Etienne P. Faana 29

Chapter 4: United States of America: Transforming Justice
Barbara J. Higdon 39

Chapter 5: Germany: The Wall Came Down
Kerstin Jeske Kristiansen and Eva Erickson 53

Chapter 6: Nigeria: Peace Is a Process Like Gardening
Joseph Charlie 62

Chapter 7: Kenya: Peace—Creating Right Order
Mary Ooko 81

Chapter 8: Democratic Republic of the Congo and Zambia:
Umutende Mukwai: Peace Please
Bunda Chibwe 89

Chapter 9: India: Peace Is Lived
Rupa Kumar 103

Chapter 10: Japan: Reflection on Peace
Hiroshi Yamada 117

Chapter 11: The Prophetic Task of Engaging with Culture
Andrew Bolton 129

Contributors 143

Introduction

This book is premised on the idea that all cultures and peoples have something to contribute to the process of peace—that deep inside us is a yearning for relationship that would connect all of humanity. These yearnings are expressed in everyday things that may be taken for granted, like a greeting: *Shalom* in Hebrew or *Announg ha shim nikka* ("Are you at peace?") in Korean. They are buried in our lullabies, our children's stories, our fables, myths, proverbs, and songs. They are reflected in stories from history and in the stories of our heroes. Those authors who would speak for us in books, theater, movies, music, and founding documents reflect them. We see them in art, symbols, logos, and sing of them in popular songs.

What do we see when we examine our ideas of peace? Is the yearning for peace only present in the poor or oppressed people who have something to gain from change, or do those with wealth and position also seek it? Who has spoken for us? Who is speaking for us now? Have other values of individual rights, strong government, possession of more land, or any number of other passions nearly snuffed out the idea of peace? What have been the barriers to peace?

How are these ideas of peace reflective of your country's geography and history? Has Christianity had an effect on the culture in regard to peace? How can the Restoration have any transforming power? What are your hopes and commitments to peace?

This book invites us to become aware of those burning rays of peace—in our own culture and in the cultures of others. These questions need to be answered, so we invite you to become part of the dialogue. We also need to understand the viewpoints of others. As the Reorganized Church of Jesus Christ of Latter Day Saints (Community of Christ) works on forming a theology of peace, let's invite all nations to be part of the dialogue. Let's learn from each other.

A special thanks goes to the authors, who put their ideas to paper for us to examine. They have each represented their own native cultures and they have done this with the background of having had a cross-cultural experience, which sharpened their insights. The authors have tackled the subject of peace in their country with great insight and, often, with brutal honesty. They have chosen their own focus, thereby creating a wonderful variety of topics.

This book can encourage each to examine the yearnings for peace within our own particular culture and stimulate the dialogue. This is only a small beginning. Other books need to be written; other conversations need to take place. We regret the limited number of countries and cultures represented here and apologize if your voice is not heard or not represented adequately. It is our hope that you will closely study the flame of peace that lights your world and share what you learn in the process.

Our theology of peace will be shaped by our relationship with the Prince of Peace. Our passion for peace for all will be acted upon out of that relationship.

"Blessed are the peacemakers, for they will be called children of God."

Darlene A. Caswell
Adult Ministries

Study Suggestions

Ask the questions we have asked above of each country you study. Learn the forces pushing toward peace and the barriers that resist it. Engage in the process by being honest in your self-reflection and open to another's perspective.

As you study each chapter find as many ways as you can to learn about the particular country and culture.

- Use a map or, preferably, a globe to locate the country and its geographic relationship to other places and to learn particular characteristics of the land.
- Try to learn as much as you can about the country's history, customs, geography, resources, language, and needs.
- Find resources on the country from the library, magazines like *National Geographic*, encyclopedias, videos, movies, and television.
- Talk to someone who has traveled or lived in the country.
- Eat foods from that country.
- Listen to the language with recordings from the library and try to pronounce the non-English words included in the text.
- Keep a vocabulary list of words from various countries with their pronunciations and meanings.

Chapter One

Assemble the Orchestra

By Howard S. Sheehy Jr.

Culture—General and Specific

In the study of anthropology—the study of human behavior in social groups—we find ourselves discussing two different elements. Some things are "culture specific," that is, a particular behavior whose meaning is found only in a particular culture; while others are "cultural general," a social behavior that appears to be almost universal in its manifestation and, while it may have some minor differences of meaning, is generally understood by all.

An example of "cultural general" may be that all mothers are protective of their children and can be expected to be alarmed and defensive when anything threatens the well-being of their child. Masai mothers in Kenya are so protective of their children that a newborn is never put down but is constantly in the arms of the mother, grandmother, or older sister. Some responsible person is consistently holding the child until he or she is nearly a year old. This would be an example of culturally specific behavior.

In some ways, peacemaking will be "culturally general" and in other ways it will be "culturally specific" behavior. This book will offer illustrations of both. The next few paragraphs will discuss a general worldview of peace.

The Orchestra

Classical music history tells us that Ludwig van Beethoven, born 1770, was composing music at the tender age of twelve and that he wrote his first orchestral symphony at age thirty. All of his early music was composed using a harpsichord, the forerunner of the piano. No one considered gathering together a full orchestra to play his music at this early age; so his first symphonies were only the sounds in his head, played out for each instrument on the harpsichord or piano. It is believed that Beethoven never heard his music in any other way because, by the time his musical genius was recognized and an orchestra was assembled to play his works, he was deaf. The sounds he heard in his head and listened to on a single instrument finally became written notes on a page to be played in future generations.

Several years ago I heard Richard Lancaster, then the director of Religious Education for the church, liken the above narrative about the life of Beethoven to the writing of the Gospels. He suggested that God had a plan, a concept about the way his children should live together. The idea, the sound or harmony that God heard in the mind, was "played out" on the single instrument of Jesus, the Christ. The life and teachings of Jesus finally became words written on a page and, after many centuries, they were assembled and took the form of the four Gospels of the New Testament.

But God's intent was not for the words to be published in the Bible. What God had in mind was to assemble the orchestra. That is, the bringing of God's children together, each playing their own unique instrument so that the human symphony, the harmony of living with love and joy together, could be heard and demonstrated for all. This book is about the "gathering" process, collecting the peacemaking patterns of many cultures so they can inform and give value to all in a new synergy for our time.

As I have had opportunity to share in ministry throughout the nations where the church has become established, and to participate in the establishment of the work in new places, I have returned over and over again to the "parable" of the orchestra. I still recall singing with the English and Welsh Saints at Dunfield House and thinking how beautifully the "violins" of God's orchestra were playing. I have felt a deep rhythm of faith in the music of French Polynesia, and with their drums and strumming I sensed a "percussion" section. I have especially enjoyed the singing of African children; their delightful harmony and counter melodies create an unusual richness that I cannot "place" in a Western orchestra. I have looked to the Orient for the reed section—quiet, subtle, yet penetrating thoughts that have the voice of the oboe and flute. I well recall a Christmas Day when Florine and I landed at the Sydney airport, arriving from New Zealand. Just after our arrival, a large group of Americans arrived from Singapore. We were struck by the noise level and the somewhat coarse and rude criticism of the airline, Australians' customs, services, immigration, and the airport layout. Nothing was right. It appeared to us that the "brass section" had arrived.

Perhaps the most universally enjoyed worship experience of the World Conference is the "hymn festival" or musical service when all of us combine our voices, our rhythms, our energy in singing the songs of faith and peace together.

The Body

The recognition of individual, as well as cultural uniqueness, is not a new idea. To the early church the apostle Paul wrote

> For as in one body we have many members, and not all the members have the same function, so we, who are many, are one body in Christ, and individually we are members one of another. We have gifts that differ according to the grace given to us: prophecy, in proportion to faith; ministry, in ministering; the teacher, in teaching; the exhorter, in exhortation; the giver, in generosity; the leader, in diligence; the compassionate, in cheerfulness. —Romans 12:4–8, New Revised Standard Version

And just before Paul's oft-quoted essay on love (I Corinthians 13) he writes:

> For just as the body is one and has many members, and all the mem-

13

bers of the body, though many, are one body, so it is with Christ. For in the one Spirit we were all baptized into one body—Jews or Greeks, slaves or free—and we were all made to drink of one Spirit.

Indeed, the body does not consist of one member but of many. If the foot would say, "Because I am not a hand, I do not belong to the body," that would not make it any less a part of the body. And if the ear would say, "Because I am not an eye, I do not belong to the body," that would not make it any less a part of the body. If the whole body were an eye, where would the hearing be? If the whole body were hearing, where would the sense of smell be? But as it is, God arranged the members in the body, each one of them, as he chose. If all were a single member, where would the body be? As it is, there are many members, yet one body. The eye cannot say to the hand, "I have no need of you," nor again the head to the feet, "I have no need of you." On the contrary, the members of the body that seem to be weaker are indispensable, and those members of the body that we think less honorable we clothe with greater honor, and our less respectable members are treated with greater respect; whereas our more respectable members do not need this. But God has so arranged the body, giving the greater honor to the inferior member, that there may be no dissension within the body, but the members may have the same care for one another. If one member suffers, all suffer together with it; if one member is honored, all rejoice together with it.

Now you are the body of Christ and individually members of it. And God has appointed in the church first apostles, second prophets, third teachers; then deeds of power, then gifts of healing, forms of assistance, forms of leadership, various kinds of tongues. Are all apostles? Are all prophets? Are all teachers? Do all work miracles? Do all possess gifts of healing? Do all speak in tongues? Do all interpret? But strive for the greater gifts. And I will show you a still more excellent way. —I Corinthians 12:12–31 NRSV

This same principle is caught up in the saying, "If all the plants in the garden were vegetables where would we find beauty; and if all the plants in the garden were flowers we would not have anything to eat."

Peacemaking Is Personal

Peacemaking is also a personal, individual act. It is often a reflection of personality or instinctive desire to create peaceful relationships.

A few years ago Florine and I took our oldest granddaughter, Amanda, then age five, with us on a ski trip to Colorado. We were staying in the condominium of some relatives. While we were there the family that owned the condo came to spend a couple of days with us. Their girls were older than Amanda and they had some school projects to work on at night after skiing. That night it was my choice to stay in with the girls while the other adults went shopping. Amanda was eager to join the "big" girls in what they were doing, but they let her know she was not welcome. Her feelings were hurt, and she came to sit with me for a little while. In about fifteen minutes she said, "Papa, will you fix me an apple?" She watched me quarter a couple of apples and put them on a plate. As soon as I was finished she took the plate to the other girls and asked them if they would like to share the apples with her. In the twinkling of an eye, and without their thinking, Amanda was part of what they were doing. She seemed to know, instinctively, how to "make peace." As a schoolgirl herself, her teacher commented on her report card, "Amanda is the peacemaker of the class. She is the first one to accept and welcome someone new and she is the one who is sensitive to the 'hurt feelings' of her classmates."

Peacemaking may be very private and personal. There is room for all to be peacemakers, in both general and specific ways.

Conclusion

As we begin a new millennium, the human family still seeks the pathway of peace. I am confident there is not just one way we shall discern peace; I am convinced there are many ways, and they are to be found among the peoples of our world. We have many values and insights to teach one another. Just as I believe that intelligence is equally shared among us, so I believe that one culture is not superior to another. We just all know different things—and only in the discovery and appreciation of the ways of peace expressed by all of God's children will we truly find ourselves building the peaceable kingdom.

For Reflection and Discussion

1. Give other examples of "culture general" and "culture specific" elements from your own or another culture. Start a two-column list (a. general, b. specific) that you can use to add examples from each chapter.

2. Listen to a short segment of a recording of an orchestra. Listen to it several times, each time listening carefully to a different section: the violins, percussion, cellos or French horns. Then discuss in what ways the orchestra is a "parable" of peacemaking.

3. In understanding the processes and practices of peace, why is it important to listen to the perspectives of people reflecting many gifts and training, temperaments, walks of life, lands and cultures?

4. What difficulties might be encountered as we try to understand another culture's viewpoint on peace? What is needed to deal with these challenges?

5. Paul reminds us that we (the church) are "the body of Christ" and are "individually members of it." Using the metaphor of the body, discuss the necessity for all parts to be present and functioning. What implications does this have on our attitudes toward the gifts of others and on how we work together?

6. Who have you known to be peacemakers? What qualities do they possess that caused you to think of them as peacemakers?

Chapter Two

Australia: How Do Australians Value Peace?

By Rick Sarre

It is difficult to say what Australians' attitudes are to peace. There are as many diverse views in Australia[1] on this subject as there are in other countries. Nevertheless, there are some issues in the social fabric of Australia that indicate that, as a whole, the nation values peace and justice and is working toward their entrenchment in a number of ways.

To illustrate the commitment that some Australians have to what I consider may be meant by the term "peace," I have selected three current policy issues drawn from my field of academic endeavor. I have chosen to discuss the notion of restorative justice, gun control (Australian-style), and the ongoing (although slow-moving) reconciliation movement linking indigenous Australians and nonindigenous Australians. Each of these examples will display something of the unique opportunities for the development of peace that currently exist in this country.

Juvenile Offenders in South Australia: Restoring Young People to Wholeness through "Restorative" Models of Justice

It was not until the mid-nineteenth century that there was a push for a separate justice system anywhere in the world for young offenders. In 1869 South Australia became the first Australian state to establish a separate system of justice for children[2] and one of the first jurisdictions in the world to legislate for a separate children's court. With this came an emphasis on treating and curing the ills that, one assumed, preordained children's aberrant behavior, rather than punishing them for their sins. A century later all states had welfare systems in place that not only dealt with juveniles under separate administrations but acted upon different (less punitive and more restorative) philosophical guidelines. The prevailing belief was that juvenile crime merely reflected problems in adolescent behavior that could be corrected through therapeutic intervention.

In November 1992 a South Australian Parliamentary Select Committee, established to look into its delivery of juvenile justice services, reported its findings. The select committee was impressed with the operation of "family group conferences" for young offenders in New Zealand, based on a Maori village justice model dating back hundreds of years. It decided to copy the notion. In 1994 a new Young Offenders Act came into operation. Under this scheme participants are invited to a family conference.[3] The offender(s), their extended families and advocates (if appropriate), the victim(s), and the police are brought together with an independent facilitator. Offenders are urged to confront their wrongdoing (for the most part less serious offences) while being allowed to develop their own negotiated outcome. The aim of the process is to bring about reconciliation and restitution, not to exact punishment or to condemn the wrongdoer without the rebuilding of social bonds. For unless these bonds are rebuilt, there may emerge ongoing and serious tensions within any community. Family conferencing is a good example of the paradigm that has come to be known as "restorative justice." Restorative justice has, as its aim, the rebuilding of broken lives and the bringing about of peace to relationships that have broken down to such an extent that the criminal justice system has become involved.[4]

Possible conference-negotiated outcomes include apologies, orders seeking up to 300 hours of community service work, financial compensation and restitution, or any other agreed measure deemed to be likely to enhance relationships and thereby deter reoffending. If there is no agreement during the conference, if the matter is very serious, or if the youth fails to appear, the case is referred to court.

There are usually four phases to the conference, although the structure is not rigid and essentially proceedings are free-flowing.

A. The conference coordinator sets out the purpose of the conference, its legal status, and the rights of each of the participants.

B. The focus then switches to the offender(s) and their supporters: how did the offence come about and what were the consequences?

C. The focus shifts to the victim(s): What was the impact of the offense on them and what were their feelings and reactions?

D. Finally, participants are directed to a discussion of what the offender ought to do to enable all those associated with the matter "to put the incident behind them" and/or to compensate or to be compensated for the harm caused.

By way of illustration, in the year 1994–1995 a total of 1,880 cases were listed for a family conference in South Australia and 1,559 were actually convened. Generally speaking, a high proportion of participants experienced successful conferences and outcomes. Some 86 percent of the undertakings were complied with. An agreement satisfactory to the parties was reached in 92 percent of cases. A survey of victim attitudes found that 93 percent of the victims contacted expressed satisfaction with the process.[5]

While one might express some doubts about the transferability of any justice program from one jurisdiction to another, the number of sites around the world—including the United States and Canada—where the idea has caught policy developers' attention indicates that the experiment has been perceived as potentially internationally adaptable.[6]

Justice programs that merely emphasize mistrust of young people and harsh retribution for those who break the law are tired and dated. "Getting tough" and "cracking down" are meaningless terms that bear little relevance to the problems tossed up to the current younger generation. Family conferences will not solve the juvenile crime problem nor the host of precipitating factors—including poverty—that allow it to persist. But the implementation of such a program might usher in a new resolve of policymakers to explore the ways the state can take into account the social milieu in which youth crime occurs and, at the same time, play a more constructive role as a broker in bringing peace and ongoing harmony to bruised and broken lives. The commitment that Australians have shown to restorative initiatives indicates an attitude to peaceful resolution, as opposed to confrontation and conflict. To that end it is a commitment to peace.

Gun Control—Australian Style

The Australian National Committee on Violence addressed the issue of firearms and violence in their 1990 report, *Violence: Directions for Australia*, a document commissioned by the Australian government following two incidents in Australia in 1987 in which armed men had killed sixteen and injured twenty-two innocent bystanders using high-powered rifles. The committee recommended major firearm restrictions. Many Australians protested, declaring their right to own a firearm. This is a field where passions run high. It is not an area where consensus is readily reached.

The committee was persuaded by the available research evidence that:

> access to firearms in Australia increased the risk of violent death both accidental and deliberate. The gun control proposals advanced by the Committee were intended to militate against any further increase in the proportion of Australians owning guns and ensure as far as possible that firearms were used only by responsible, skilled shooters. The Committee

expressed the view that firearms ownership was a privilege not a right and that the strict controls they proposed would impress upon the public that firearms were inherently dangerous.[7]

The most vehement opposition at the time to the committee's proposals came from political representatives of the Australian states of Queensland, New South Wales, and Tasmania. These three states, a year later, walked away from talks on a national licensing system. The political climate was alive with heated debate. Noted gun-lobby activists made trips to the United States, and NRA (National Rifle Association) representatives traveled to Australia. Some alleged that they provided finance for their Australian counterparts. Some Australians began to speak of conspiracy theories and referred to the "right to bear arms," trademark language in the war of words in the United States.

The events at Tasmania's idyllic tourist destination at Port Arthur in April 1996, when a disturbed young loner named Martin Bryant killed thirty-five people in less than an hour, reversed this mindset in a matter of two weeks. Indeed, within four months of the shooting spree a gun "buy-back" scheme was a reality. The handing in of all semiautomatic and all unregistered weapons to Australian authorities began on September 30, 1996, exactly one year ahead of the day when the possession of a banned weapon became a criminal offense[8]. By the time the pro-gun lobbies had mustered their forces, the prime minister's program had all but been completed.[9] By August 1998 a total of 643,726 semiautomatic rifles and pump-action shotguns had been surrendered for incineration at a cost to the Australian taxpayer of almost $200 million (U.S.).

In the entire debate surrounding this topic, however, there has been a distinct inability by either "side" to point to persuasive evidence of the effectiveness of such controls one way or the other. Hard data and statistically significant studies are difficult to obtain and construct. Advocates on both sides of the gun divide in Australia make sweeping statements that assume that relationships between guns and violence or guns and safety are well documented and understood. They are not. We are deep in the realms of uncertainty. Arguments in both directions are based on little more than faith and preconceived ideological positions. In North America, Gabor[10] arrived at the conclusion that firearm ownership and homicide rates are positively related, given their lethality, danger to bystanders, and amenability to drive-by shootings. But his findings have not been replicated in Australia, although there is some evidence that restricting the availability of firearms reduces firearm-related deaths.[11]

There are many variables that impact firearm death rates. Firearm (indeed semiautomatic firearm) availability is just one of the variables. The links between gun availability and gun deaths remain unclear. Comparisons that may be useful are the gun homicide rates between countries. Firearm homicides in Australia are about two per 100,000 population, compared to the American figure that is almost ten per 100,000.[12]

Gun ownership is a privilege not a right, and the lives of many individuals are at risk of violent death when restrictions on ownership and use (outside of legitimate fields such as the military) are lifted or relaxed. The Australia Region of the Re-organized Church at its Easter 1999 conference passed a resolution calling on the church to encourage its membership, as an act of stewardship, to renounce the personal use of guns, mirroring a similar resolution of the 210th General Assembly of the Presbyterian Church (USA) in 1998.

The greatest resistance to the buy-back scheme appears to have come from urban recreational shooters, those who, one might assume, have the least genuine need to own such a weapon. The avalanche of support for the prime minister's initiative ensured that one of the most radical reforms in Australia's recent social history came about quickly and with little partisan acrimony. Australians appear committed to peace from firearms.

Reconciliation between Indigenous and Nonindigenous Australians

Indigenous peoples inhabited the Australian continent for up to 60,000 years before explorers from other lands first began visiting our shores more than 300 years ago. Indigenous Australians enjoyed their own forms of government. Their "Dreaming" stories told of their relationships with their creator, the environment, and each other and explained their responsibilities as custodians of the land, waters, and resources for future generations. Their tribes spoke upwards of 200 languages and 600 dialects.

Sadly, the effects of enforced monoculturalism over two centuries since colonization has led to the demise of indigenous spiritual and legal restraints and drastically eroded the security, cultural integrity, and self-esteem of indigenous peoples. In the past decades there has been no shortage of evidence to show the need to improve health, education, and employment for indigenous Australians. Commission after commission, study after study, have concluded that indigenous Australians are at vastly greater risk of threat to life and health than nonindigenous Australians. Indigenous Australians, who make up only 2 percent of the Australian population, face the risk of becoming a victim of homicide, for example, at a rate far greater than that borne by the general Australian population. In the period 1989–1996 more than 18 percent of homicide offenders were indigenous Australians; 14 percent of homicide victims were indigenous. Indigenous Australians have a life expectancy fifteen to seventeen years lower than nonindigenous Australians, and infant mortality stands at more than twice the rate applying to the national population taken as a whole.

Unfortunately, our history with respect to the treatment of indigenous people is not something in which the current generation of Australians can take pride. Attitudes of racial, theological, and cultural superiority led to a suppression of indigenous culture, religion, and values. There is little doubt why Australia's first colonists developed racist attitudes and passed them so confidently to succeeding generations. Note what the international European jurist Vattel wrote in 1758:

> There is another celebrated question which has arisen principally in connection with the discovery of the New World. It is asked whether a Nation may lawfully occupy any part of a vast territory in which are to be found only wandering tribes whose small numbers cannot populate the whole country....[W]hen the Nations of Europe, which are too confined at home, come upon lands which the savages have no special need of, and are making no present and continuous use of, they may lawfully take possession of them and establish colonies in them....[W]e are not departing from the intersections of nature when we restrict the savages within narrower bounds.[13]

Fortunately, things have moved on from this official eighteenth-century legal position. Australia is not only a signatory of the Universal Declaration on Human Rights but also the International Covenant on Civil and Political Rights (ICCPR, signed by Australia on December 18, 1972), the Convention on the Prevention and Punishment of the Crime of Genocide (signed by Australia on December 11, 1948), the International Convention on the Elimination of All Forms of Racial Discrimination (signed by Australia on October 13, 1966), and the International Covenant on Economic, Social and Cultural Rights (signed by Australia on December 18, 1972) which, collectively, establish a moral and legal basis for the recognition of indigenous rights in this country.[14]

Despite this creditworthy international record, disenfranchisement of indigenous peoples continued well into the twentieth century and well past the time when Australia had been a signatory to some of the above-mentioned international human rights conventions. Indigenous Australians could not vote in federal elections until as recently as 1962. It was not until 1967 that indigenous people were counted in a census. For 150 years (into the 1970s) the governments of this country removed indigenous children from their families in order to "save" them from not being brought up in respectable homes and Christian families. The consequences of these policies in terms of broken families, shattered health, loss of language, culture, and connection to traditional land, loss of parenting skills, and distress has now been brought to the attention of Australians by the "Stolen Generation" report.

There are some encouraging signs. The number of deaths of indigenous Australians in police custody has dropped significantly in the last five years. Life expectancy is on the increase. Nevertheless, it is overdue for Australians to strive more actively to promote conditions more conducive to peace between indigenous and nonindigenous races, especially in relation to responding to the "Stolen Generation" report. It is imperative that Australians continue to embrace the notion of reconciliation and acknowledge past wrongs with an apology. A number of churches (not ours) have officially called on governments in Australia to acknowledge blame for past practices, but the realization of this dream is slow in coming. The Quaker Society has made their peace with the original custodians of our land, as did the Uniting Church in September 1996. The Anglican Church at its 11th General Synod in 1998 apologized unreservedly to indigenous peoples and sought forgiveness "for any part played, knowingly or unwittingly, by the Anglican Church that has ever contributed in any way to [the] hurt or trauma by the unjustified removal of Indigenous or Torres Strait Islander children from their families, and for our past silence on the issue."

We, as a church, I believe, watched without understanding as decisions were made that had the effect of weakening the identity of indigenous peoples, suppressing their languages and cultures, and outlawing their spiritual practices. We, as a church, could now recognize the impact of these actions and inactions and express our deepest regret. Despite efforts by the Australian Human Rights and Equal Opportunity Commission to commit Australians to a path of forgiveness and reconciliation, the road appears to have been paved with little more than good intentions. Reconciliation is an ongoing process. In renewing our partnership with all Australians, we must ensure that the mistakes that marked our past relationship are not repeated. The church must commit itself to working with like organizations to achieve shared goals that will benefit all Australians, indigenous and nonindigenous alike, and by so doing bring about a peaceful coexistence.

Conclusion

What can we say about Australians and peace? I have illustrated, by the use of these three examples, that the essence of peace can be found in societal practices and paradigms in our day-to-day lives. Some stories are positive, and some are less so. I am of the view that the current juvenile justice system (if not the adult system) could enhance its credibility and success rate by focusing less on deterrence and retribution—essentially violent concepts—and more on the opportunities for victim and offender to seek reconciliation. This has been shown by the "conferencing" model of restorative justice that has been established successfully in most Australian states and is now being copied in other parts of the world. I believe the control of firearms can be viewed as a peace-based stewardship principle. The Australian gun-control experience provides a positive policy model. Finally, Australia's experiment with reconciliation between races, while burdened with a history of violence against indigenous owners of the land at the time of the first colonists and since, is not yet a success story. The door must now be opened more widely on a process of reconciliation with all indigenous peoples in Australia to reduce the current levels of tension, and remove the conditions that give rise to health and criminal justice statistics that overwhelmingly discriminate in favor of nonindigenous Australians.

Each of these initiatives—restorative justice, gun control, and racial reconciliation—provides concrete examples of Australia's commitment to the tasks and responsibilities necessary to the pursuit of peace into the next century.

For Reflection and Discussion

1. How are juvenile offenders treated in your community? How is it the same or different from adult offenders? How would you like to see it improved?

2. What elements of the "restorative justice" model outlined by the author make a more positive outcome possible?

3. What do you feel the church can and should do to prevent the occurrences of juvenile crime? What ministry can the church give after crimes are committed?

4. Role-play being participants in the Australian Region's discussion of the Easter 1999 resolution on firearms, bringing out any points you would have wanted them to consider.

5. What do you see as the basic issues at stake in the gun control debate? How do you see the gospel of Jesus Christ relating to these basic issues? How should the church respond?

6. What do you draw from your understanding of the gospel that informs you how to behave toward other groups of people that have different beliefs and practices?

7. In what other places in the world have there been adjustments to be made between immigrants and indigenous people? What were the outcomes in these places?

8. What insights did you gain from this chapter? (Keep this list to add insights from other chapters.)

Notes

1. Currently 18 million people call Australia home on a landmass about the size of the continental United States. It has a coastline of some 20,000 miles, an official language of English (although more than 130 languages are spoken, including a dozen surviving indigenous languages), and government by a parliamentary constitutional monarchist system. Australia has become one of the most multicultural nations on earth—

four in ten Australians are immigrants or children of immigrants—and its indigenous population has a history on this island continent dating back some sixty millennia.

2. At the time, anyone under twenty-one years of age, now anyone under eighteen years of age.

3. Police issue the invitation if they think it an appropriate case, but a magistrate may override this decision.

4. The responsibility of restorative justice is made more urgent given facts such as those reported in December 1996 by the National Center for Children in Poverty at Columbia University, that 25 percent of children in the United States now live in families with incomes below the poverty line, the highest percentage of any industrialized Western nation.

5. Victims chose to be present in only 49 percent of cases.

6. Rick Sarre, "Family Conferencing as a Juvenile Justice Strategy," *The Justice Professional* 4, no. 11 (1999): 259–271.

7. D. Chappell, "Buying Back the Arsenal: The On-Going Saga of Antipodean Gun Law Reform," unpublished paper presented to the American Society of Criminology, Chicago (November 23, 1996), 6.

8. The National Firearm Monitoring program monitors the Nationwide Agreement on Firearms, which bans self-loading rifles, self-loading and pump-action shotguns, and introduces a nationwide registration system of firearms and firearm ownership.

9. Rick Sarre, "Gun Control in Australia," 21 (4) (December 1997): 412–418. Refer also to Rick Sarre, "What Can be Done About Violence?" in Wayne Ham, ed., *Restoration Studies VI* (Independence, Missouri: Herald House, 1995), 169–177.

10. T. Gabor, *The Impact of the Availability of Firearms on Violent Crime, Suicide, and Accidental Death: a Review of the Literature with Special Reference to the Canadian Situation*, Department of Justice, Canada (1994), 35.

11. *Australian Bureau of Statistics Firearm Deaths Australia 1980–1995*, ABS Cat. No. 4397.0.

12. M. James and C. Carcach, "Homicide in Australia 1989–1996" *Research and Public Policy Series* No. 13, Australian Institute of Criminology, Canberra (1997).

13. E. de Vattel, *The Law of Nations*, 1758, English Translation by G. Fenwick (New York, Oceana Publications,1964), chapter 18, paragraph 209, page 85.

14. Refer Rick Sarre, "The Imprisonment of Indigenous Australians: Dilemmas and Challenges for Policy-makers," *Georgetown Public Policy Review*, (Forthcoming 1999).

Chapter Three

French Polynesia: Hau, Aroha, Peace

By Etienne P. Faana

The subject of peace from a Pacific historical and cultural perspective is a complex issue that cannot be adequately treated in this short paper. I humbly admit that there are no resources by indigenous professional researchers available to us in Tahiti that treat the issue of peace. What is available is by social anthropologists and ethnologists such as Dr. Robert Levy, Douglas Oliver, Jane and James Ritchie, and others from whom this paper was prepared. The Polynesians are indebted to these social scientists who have contributed their expertise as it relates to the Polynesian cultural community thought pattern and form and the issue of peace. Their work covers the pre-Christian era to the modern era of the Polynesian culture.

For the Pacific people, peace continues to be a process and a dynamic form that is to be understood in the current economical, social, religious, and political arena in which modern Polynesia is trying to relate today and in this new millennium.

Peace—*Hau*—as a Form of Government within the Polynesian Worldview

Douglas Oliver in *Ancient Tahitian Society*[1] relates peace to the Tahitian word "*hau*" (pronounced haoo). He indicated that *hau* (peace) is rooted in the secular aspect of the tribal chieftain. In this research he isolated *hau* as a secular aspect, isolating it from the religious. This tendency of dualism is part of the Western cultural worldview while in Polynesian culture secular and religious are intrinsically related—they are one.

He indicated that the LMS (London Missionary Society, a religious Western institution that first Christianized the Polynesians) dictionary suggested that there are three forms of entries for peace/hau: (1.) the dew that falls at night, (2.) government, and (3.) reign. In the tribal chieftain political structure, peace is closely related to reign or government. It is also related to the notion of "war" (*tama'i*, pronounced tahmah-e). Viewed in this context, *hau* is connected with religious thought form relating to a cosmogonic myth of the Polynesian creation story. *Taaro'a* (Tahahroah), the Polynesian creator, fashioned the world and placed his right eye in *Atea* (Ah ta-ah), Venus, who runs in the evening and said, "It is to be a light before the earth to lead it to give great peace [Hau'Hau], 'Peace to the inhabited world.'" Here peace refers to the institutional social structure of government. "Inhabited world" signifies government, the peace, the hau, in this context.

Douglas Oliver further indicates that following a time of war and the resanctification of a community after the defeat and devastation of war, a Polynesian priest is heard on the *marae* (mahrah, a Polynesian open temple and sanctuary) saying a prayer: "'*Fano ei hau, e hau rahi. Ei hau hohonu, ei hau maoro, ei hau maitai roa'* Extend forth peace, great peace. Let it be deep peace, long peace, excellent peace."[2]

In the speeches that accompanied truce negotiations, the decision for peace was demonstrated by throwing a rock onto the ground followed by these chanted speeches:

> There is the rock for peace,
> the rocks of the body of warriors,
> the rock for sparing men,
> that the land may flourish.
> Send forth the heralds to proclaim peace.

Let there be peace, long unbroken peace.
Let peace be in the dwellings of the people.[3]

It is further interesting to note, indicates Oliver, that there is also a "spirit of peace/hau" identified as a god of peace, characterized as a tutelar or guardian of medical specialists named *"Tahu'a raau"* (medicinal priest). However, peace, in our current exposé is mostly related to a form of "government, of people, of chieftain kinship" closely related to "war." There are numerous examples and legends in the Polynesian culture whereby "peace and war" are interrelated. Peace/hau can also be related to "a king's kingdom or kingly government," the *Haumanahune* meaning the government of the common people, a form of democracy. In order to maintain peaceful treaty or peaceful cohabitation among neighboring islands against hostile island tribes, a peace alliance called *"Hau-Pahu-Nui"* (Government of the Great Drum) is restored and respected. This form of "peace alliance" was in force until the end of the nineteenth century and it remained in full force until French rule was permanently established in Tahiti in 1847.[4] Alliance in the Polynesian cultural context means: *fa'ataua,* to make a friend.

The above information indicates to us that peace/hau represents for the *Maohis* (indigenous term for Polynesians) thoughts of the tribal and religious aspect of their lives. However, according to Oliver, the tribal aspect of peace/hau cannot be divorced from the social order of the community as a whole.

It is in this area that the works of Jane and James Ritchie are of great value to us as we try to relate to the RLDS concept of peace in our day.

Peace—Hau—As a Form of Social and Dynamic Structure within the Polynesian Worldview

Studies conducted by Jane and James Ritchie[5] on the formation of the Polynesian character and socialization during the pre-Christian era indicated that "group life and community identity" maintains some form of "social, political, and religious" equilibrium within the community. That equilibrium entertains a spirit of peace within it. They also indicated that warfare is another cultural element that needs to be considered in light of the "security and survival" of the communal life of the village. In this context, remark the Ritchies, warfare is not so much considered as political dominion over an enemy territory, but rather as an element to support the formation of that "communal identity, spirit of cohesiveness" against "intra-group rivalries and hostility." In order to maintain "peaceful equilibrium" within the community or the village life, warfare is regarded as a necessity.[6] Therefore, the Ritchies contend the Polynesian worldview on "peace and war" during the pre-Christian era (and this is perhaps true today) is quite different from the Western worldview of peace and war.

Peace and war or "just war" thought form from the *popaa* (white man) perspective may be quite different from the Polynesian thought form and pattern. Certainly, there has been warfare between different island tribes during the pre-Christian era. However, as noted by the Ritchies, it was not for "political dominion nor conquering ambition nor for power hunger" but rather to maintain the "the peaceful cohesiveness, identity and security" of the tribe and life of the community. I believe that sentiment still exists today within the major Polynesian islands throughout the Pacific.

It is generally recognized and acknowledged that group identity, social equilibrium, equality, the spirit of generosity, of care, of group support are indeed important elements of the Polynesian character and culture. It is within this characterization that peace is maintained. Warfare in economic competitiveness, individual glorification, materialism, and geopolitical dominion of the *"popaa World"* (the white man) are totally alien to the Polynesian character.[7]

Polynesians are totally "disarmed," noted the Ritchies, and will demonstrate a traumatic and emotional state of disposition when taken away from their "community environment" and are placed in a totally "alien" environment. Generally speaking a Polynesian is afraid of "solitude and loneliness," desiring to be constantly connected with his or her group environment at all times. It is within that "group connection, identity, social structure, and support" that the Polynesian finds peace.[8]

In traditional Polynesia, and perhaps this may be true in some traditional island people in the Pacific today, the world of the *popaa*, the white man, may present an obstacle to them by the very nature of their character structure. For as I indicated earlier, the world of the *popaa* for success depends on fighting, striving, ambition, aggressiveness, thrift, long-range planning, and on individual responsibility.

Does this mean that Polynesians are unable to adapt to a new environment? Studies by the Ritchies further indicated that in the pre-Christian era, there was migration and colonization of islands by the earlier Polynesian migrators.[9] These colonies were able to reinvent their cultures over and over again, and they reinvent their history accordingly.[10] Cultures that have the capacity to assimilate the "new" must contain ways of validating and valuing individual departures from orthodoxy. They must train people to have a high level of tolerance for ambiguity and to suspend judgment, as well as to educate people in the creative use of conflict. Whereas other cultures deal with conflict by seeking to dissolve differences and to find ultimate solutions, Polynesians have historically chosen to incorporate differences, and to use them as a means of keeping options open. Polynesian cultures thus represent adaptations to conflicting interests, overlapping allegiances, and multiple solutions to every problem. For Polynesians any or all solutions are tentative, subject to reformulation as conditions change.[11]

Let me give you a vivid illustration. In modern French Polynesia, particularly on the island of Tahiti, the Evangelical Church (the predominant Protestant Christian denomination) is considered to be the "preserver" of the Polynesian traditional values of the pre-Christian era. It is interesting to note that during major religious celebrative events, all pastors and religious leaders wore their "European style appararel: black suits, white shirts, and ties" (Western Christian colonial style), while the women wore "long white dress and white hats" (depicting the European long dress and white hat style) but the entire liturgy and services were "very traditional."[12]

This is to indicate that these are ways of demonstrating they are technologically and modernly "hip" while at the same time their songs and services emphasize traditional themes and concerns. It does indicate further the "peaceful cohabitation" of the old and the new, reemphasizing the ability of the Polynesians to assimilate the "new" while they, at the same time, "hold on to tradition."

This "peaceful form of cohabitation" of two worldviews in modern Polynesia is further reinforced by kinship relatedness as a model for "inclusiveness."[13] Each person in a Polynesian community can be incorporated into every other's kinship network; even incorporating an "alien person" into the kinship network is very common. For example, a *popaa* person (white person) married to a native Polynesian person (male or female) is automatically incorporated into the kinship network. A common and popular illustration relates to the wedding celebration event. The "alien bride or groom," during the celebration feast, will be given a "Polynesian name" that relates them to a common and popular kinship hero or king or queen. The "alien person" will therefore be called by the entire community by that name alone.[14]

Another important factor that needs to be noted in this cultural dynamic relates to "sharing and caring."[15] It is the duty of the *"Ariki"* (king or Polynesian aristocracy) to care for the poor. The authority of the *Ariki* is tested when he or she demonstrates in a concrete sense his or her *"Oha, Aroha"* (love, compassion, caring) in the service of "relationship." *Oha, Aroha* is a powerful concept of sharing, of giving (today it is the giving of money) for the benefit of "peaceful cohabitation and relationship."

Jane and James Ritchie indicate further that to maintain

"peaceful relationship," unity through consensus is to be acknowledged.[16] To the Western mind a dual emphasis on status rivalry and consensus politics may appear paradoxical, but not for the Polynesians. For Polynesians consensus is valued because it enhances community. Even these days when the phenomenal reality of community may be fractured or in decline—particularly in urbanized areas—people still speak as though all actions should be related to a cohesive community. It matters not if one's relatives are elsewhere.

In an urban Polynesian community, any individual achievements must be accompanied by "humility," a sense of acknowledgment of the cultural community value. This maintains a healthy "peaceful relationship" toward the entire community.

Does Polynesian culture acknowledge individual achievements? Yes. Polynesians admire individuals who express a strong sense of independence while acknowledging community consensus, who are able to fulfill the obligations of membership in a community with generosity and humility, and who can tolerate conflict and ambiguity while adapting to change.

Therefore the concepts of *"Oha, Koha, Oha Oha,* and *Aroha"* are central to the Polynesian "ethos." They provide the basic formation for the Polynesian worldview. *"Koha, Oha, Oha, and Aroha"* can be translated into "sharing, giving, love, compassion, caring"; it is within this form of the Polynesian ethos that peace is to be understood.

In Conclusion

How does all this relate to the mission of the church for the twenty-first century with regard to becoming an international church for the "pursuit of peace, reconciliation, and healing of the Spirit?" There are key elements in Polynesian culture as it relates to peace. Let me enunciate some of these elements based on our reflection from the Polynesian peace perspective:

• Peace within the government and rules of the church hierarchical system should be in service to the community.

- Peace is to be lived concretely, not in concept alone but in concrete demonstration for the community's sake.
- A "theology of relationship" is expressed in the Polynesian peace concept, "connectedness support."
- Inclusiveness and kinship incorporation are basic to the Polynesian value "to make a friend (peace alliance)" or "friendship."
- Strong emphasis on the "theology of community" is expressed in the RLDS concept of Zionic community, "togetherness."
- Humility in politics and personal achievements emphasizes community welfare rather than "personal glorification."
- Most of all, *aroha*—which denotes the entire Polynesian cultural and social and political dynamics—can be translated in our church context as *peace=hau/aroha,* "government of peace and love, a community of peace and love, a community of *shalom.*"

Aroha is relationship. Aroha is peace. Aroha is compassion. Aroha is caring. Aroha is giving. Aroha is humility. Aroha is respect. Aroha is equality. Aroha is justice. Aroha is community. Aroha is all! Aroha comes from the "bottom of one's entire being." Aroha is "being." Aroha is peace and justice and reconciliation and healing.

Pronunciation of Polynesian Words and Meaning

Aroha (Ahrofah): peace, love, compassion, caring, sharing, etc.
Oha (Ohfah): same
Hau (Haoo): peace in the war and government context
Koha (Kohfah): love, compassion, caring, etc.
Ariki (AhReekee): king, chief
Popaa (Pohpah ah): white person
Maohi (Mah Oh Hee): native Polynesian
Hau Pahu Nui (Hah oo Pah hoo Noo ee): Government of the Great Drum

Hau Mana Hune (Ha oo Mah nah Hoo nay): government of the
   common people
Ta'ataua (Tah ah tah oo ah) to make a friend

For Reflection and Discussion

1. Experience the sound of the Tahitian language by pronouncing aloud the words the author has provided for you. In what
ways would learning the language of another culture help the
establishment of peace? Is there a word you would like to add
to your international peace vocabulary?

2. The author points out the Western tendency toward "dualistic" thinking that separates and thinks in opposites—like "ei-
ther/or," rather than "both/and." Discuss how dualistic or
nondualistic thinking might affect the search for peace.

3. According to Douglas Oliver's contention that peace or "hau"
has much to do with how people organize themselves in a social order, what might be called government? In what ways does
social order relate to peace?

4. Explain how the Polynesian view of war is different from
the Western practice of war.

5. From reading this chapter, describe what you believe to be
important values to the Polynesians.

6. Discuss how each of the following helps to create peace in
community:
   a. peaceful cohabitation of the old and new;
   b. kinship relatedness;
   c. caring and sharing of the "Arkiki";
   d. consensus; and
   e. humility about one's achievements.

7. Which of the author's insights on Polynesian culture is most
appealing and challenging to you? Explain why.

Notes

1. Douglas Oliver, *Ancient Tahitian Society,* 2 (Honolulu, Hawaii: University of Hawaii, 1993), 1049–1053.
2. Ibid, 321.
3. Ibid, 1050.
4. Ibid, 1052.
5. Jane and James Ritchie, *Socialization and Character Development,* (Honolulu, Hawaii: University of Hawaii, 1993), 95–120.
6. Ibid, 98.
7. Ibid, 99.
8. Ibid.
9. Ibid, 101–102.
10. Alan Howard and Robert Borofsky, *Development in Polynesian Ethnology* (Honolulu, Hawaii: University of Hawaii, 1993), Introduction by Dr. Robert I. Levy, University of San Diego, California.
11. Ibid.
12. Robert I. Levy, *The Tahitians* (Chicago: Chicago Press, 1973).
13. Ritchie, 104–105.
14. Personal Testimonies, Sanito Church Wedding Celebration Feast, Tahiti, French Polynesia.
15. Ritchie, 107.
16. Ritchie, 110–113.

Chapter Four

United States of America: Transforming Justice

By Barbara J. Higdon

Recent headlines announce a startling departure from traditional ways of doing business; the governor of California will remove a controversial proposition approved by voters from the judicial appeals process and submit it for mediation. In doing so he opts for a relatively new, but promising technique for solving a contentious dispute over the presence of illegal immigrants in California public schools. Opponents have challenged his choice of mediation, as well as the issues raised by the appeal of the legality of the proposition. The use of mediation is not usually an additional issue in the disputes where it is employed; in fact, its efficacy as a peacemaking opportunity is recognized by many individuals and communities.

In the United States the Alternative Dispute Resolution movement (ADR) is exerting a slow but steady influence on the way conflict is resolved. Most of the new practices—many of them developed within the last ten years—are supplementing or replacing old, less productive ways of dealing with the inevitable disputes that arise as human beings interact within the relational framework of societal structures—in families, neighborhoods, workplaces, bureaucracies, even in international diplomacy. ADR incorporates principles and practices that present alternatives to the aggressive, litigious, combative style that has characterized the national culture of the United States. A cherished tradition of individualism with its promise of personal success to anyone who works the hardest, overcomes all obstacles—including human ones—and keeps an eye single to the glory of the goal is one of the most important factors explaining the violence of our culture. Our everyday language reflects the win-lose perspective of sports and war, and, in an environment of plentiful resources, we have one of the highest rates of violent crime in the world.

Although the judicial process is the time-honored method for dealing with disputes, Americans have a love-hate relationship with the system and its practitioners. From our national beginnings we have had a deep-seated distrust of lawyers. In our own time, we need look no further than the numerous lawyer jokes to document the lack of respect and antagonism with which lawyers are held by many people until, that is, a trained guide is needed to lead us through the legal maze of divorce, lawsuit, or estate disposition. In addition to the legal needs of the individual, regulatory federal and state legislation has spawned an avalanche of actions concerning disputes relating to civil rights, the environment, and business relationships. That perceptive French observer of American culture, Alexis de Tocqueville, wrote in 1835: "Scarcely any political question arises in the United States that is not resolved, sooner or later, into a judicial question."

Even though lay persons have been heard to mutter Shakespeare's injunction to "kill all the lawyers" and have enjoyed a laugh at the expense of their attorneys, we know that our judicial system has served individuals and society well. Courts repeatedly have broken new ground in establishing important precedents in support of the less powerful members of our society. Ethnic minorities, women, children, and people with disabilities have found not only protection but support for equal opportunities to develop their individual potential. The courtroom increasingly has become the venue where individuals have a chance to voice their complaints against powerful institutions.

For all of its faults—among which the advantage wealthy individuals enjoy looms large—the legal system of the United States has been an important and positive influence in our history.

However, the judicial system certainly contains the defects of its qualities. Costly procedures with enormous front-end overhead expenses and long delays have made it anything but "user friendly." Derek Bok, former president of Harvard University and former dean of the Harvard Law School, criticized his profession as "strewn with the disappointed hopes of those who find [it] too complicated to understand, too quixotic to command respect, and too expensive to be of much practical use." His colleague at Harvard Law, Laurence Tribe, summarized the system's problems as follows: "Too much law, too little justice; too many rules, too few results...."

Perhaps its most serious disadvantage in the late twentieth century, which has rearticulated the importance of human community, is its adversarial structure that requires a win-lose outcome. The resulting inevitable destruction of preexisting relationships between people is judged by today's values to be a high human cost indeed. Although the judicial system plays an important and unique role in our society which has benefited immeasurably from its influence and will continue to do so in the future, for some classes of disputes new ways of resolution have been designed and are being practiced with remarkable success.

Before describing some of these new systems and their antecedents, it may be instructive to examine some sources of the late twentieth-century emphasis on the importance of maintaining and nurturing human relationships. Sociologists will spend years identifying and analyzing the myriad influences that have modified U.S. society in the direction of a kinder, gentler community. Of the many cultural forces working to reduce the divisive consequences of conflict on people and communities, three deserve special mention because of the impact they have had on large numbers of people in the United States: the feminist movement; the Program on Negotiation at Harvard Law

41

School; and the work of two individuals, Stephen Covey and M. Scott Peck. Each of these influences has emphasized principles that are incorporated in the philosophy of alternative dispute resolution.

The Feminist Movement

The most pervasive and general of the three influences on conflict resolution is the feminist movement. Even though in its role as change agent it has created significant social upheaval, from its beginnings it has claimed a constructive role in addressing conflict. The feminist criticism of the patriarchal structure of society in which men dominate women and children stimulated a creative look at traditional habits of relationships between people, not just between men and women. The classic process of dispute resolution practiced today draws important principles and practices from the experiences of the feminist movement: acknowledgment of mutual responsibility for the conflict, recognition of different styles of moral reasoning about conflicts, and egalitarian practices of human interaction.

Gerda Lerner maintains that in the social arrangement of patriarchy men are not offenders and women are not victims, but that both are responsible participants. Thus they are both responsible for redressing the wrong and devising alternative visions. Mediation encourages disputants to take responsibility for their problem and its solution.

Without judging one as better than the other, Carol Gilligan has identified two gender-specific styles of moral reasoning— an "ethics of justice" favored by males and an "ethics of care" favored by females. Recognizing the clash of thinking styles and the different priorities that result from these styles is an important element of formal conflict resolution. Behaviors promoted in feminist consciousness-raising groups incorporated respectful and supportive behaviors: topics moved from less to more sensitive issues; conversation flowed from participant to participant with no one person leading; no speaker was to be

42

interrupted; no one's contribution was to be minimized; and accurate summaries reflected the content of individual contributions. These practices have been regularized in classic mediation practices.

Harvard Negotiation Project

The Harvard Negotiation Project consists of research, teaching, and negotiation services. A consortium of scholars from major universities has worked for thirty years developing, refining, and disseminating the theory and practice of conflict resolution. The project has developed programs for lawyers, businesspeople, diplomats, journalists, government officials, union leaders, and military officers. Graduate and undergraduate students learn techniques and participate in research. A pilot curriculum for high-school students has also been developed. The methods recommended by the center played an important role in the successful Middle East peace negotiations at Camp David in 1978. "Principled negotiation" described in the bestselling book, *Getting to Yes* by Roger Fisher and William Ury, recommends that disputants learn how to separate people from problems thus resolving issues on their merits, focusing on interests not positions in order to discover options containing mutual benefits, and insisting that outcomes be based on fair standards, employing objective criteria independent of the will of either side.

The center has developed a wide variety of publications for use by practitioners, teachers, and students, including material on international negotiations. An important source of raw material for the center's research is the ongoing conflict over public issues whose participants are sometimes invited to bring their experience to the center's scholars. The work of the center has had a tremendous influence on the practice of conflict resolution in the United States and abroad.

Peck and Covey

The publications and workshops sponsored by M. Scott Peck and Stephen Covey have broadly disseminated principles employed in formal conflict resolution. Peck has suggested ways in which recognizing problems and working to resolve them can help people reach a higher level of understanding of self and others. In his books, especially *The Road Less Traveled,* he has called for a greater degree of individual responsibility for personal growth. His methods of resolving internal conflict are similar to the methods of classic conflict resolution. In his work in community development, he advocates group responsibility for more human and supportive human communities.

Stephen Covey's *The 7 Habits of Highly Effective People* presents a rough diagram and sequence for the mediator. Even though Covey has not addressed himself to the ADR movement directly, each of his seven habits is applicable and reinforces the philosophy followed by the mediator and the disputants who seek the help of mediation to solve their conflicts. Habit 1, "Be proactive," advises people to take responsibility for their own lives, for their reactions, for their choices of action. Habit 2, "Begin with the end in mind," suggests an imaginative, unrestricted invention of outcomes. Habit 3, "Put first things first," emphasizes the importance of identifying the basic values that motivate the behavior of an individual. Although not the first person to use the phrase, Covey's Habit 4, "Think win/win" seeks to discover mutual benefit in human interaction. Habit 5, "Seek first to understand, then to be understood," prescribes careful and deep empathic listening to other people and clear, specific, contextual presentation to others of a person's own ideas. Habit 6, "Synergize," describes the creativity that occurs when people are free to cooperatively explore new and untried solutions to problems and challenges including disputes. Habit 7, "Sharpen the saw," addresses personal renewal that results from the practice of the other six.

Alternative Dispute Resolution

The feminist movement and Covey's and Peck's ideas are powerful expressions of themes present in late twentieth-century U.S. culture that have influenced and been influenced by a strong concern for individual empowerment and a vision of peace and justice. The Alternative Dispute Resolution movement belongs to that cultural theme.

Not only has the ADR movement been influenced by relatively recent popular ideas, but it also draws from older traditions of religious and immigrant populations—early settlers from England, Holland, Scandinavia, and China, as well as Jewish immigrants from western Europe. Rather than resorting to the legal system in the days of the village in our early history, church or community leaders would serve as a focal point in the solution of conflicts.

An important formalization of the concept occurred in 1947 when the U.S. Congress created the Federal Mediation and Conciliation Service as an independent agency to settle labor disputes, building on the records of earlier publicly sponsored agencies created for the purpose of dealing with labor disputes. A movement led by attorneys who feared that increasing pressure on the courts would eventually break the legal system began to search for and advocate alternative dispute resolution practices.

Various models have been employed by a great many groups within U.S. society: businesses, families, enforcement agencies, public schools, federal agencies, local and state officials. Law schools, universities, and social service agencies are training mediators, and individuals are setting up private mediation practices. Professional associations and international conferences are beginning to create canons of ethics, review current research, and establish networks of teachers and practitioners.

Although mediation practices and structures vary widely, certain benefits and outcomes set the movement apart from the traditional legal system. Mediation is not appropriate for all disputes. It cannot replace the legal process by which lawbreak-

45

ers are convicted and punished, for example. However mediation has a number of benefits for dealing with certain kinds of conflict. It is almost always faster and cheaper than the judicial system. Because disputants must take an active, direct role in solving their problem, they experience greater satisfaction in the feeling of control that this direct involvement brings. Collaboration between people in conflict in devising their own solutions often creates more creative and satisfactory outcomes and will frequently preserve the personal relationship between the parties. Finally, people who have played a direct and active role in solving their problems are much more likely to abide by the agreements reached than if they have been ordered to conform to a settlement imposed by a third party.

The Mediation Process

Although the mediation process varies slightly from trainer to trainer, the philosophy and basic principles are similar. The system described here is common. Differences usually would reflect a difference in the nature of the dispute and whether an unalterable imbalance of power existed between the disputants, such as in a parent/child conflict. Mediators must be trained to manage and direct the mediation process as follows:

1. **Introduction:** Co-mediators explain the process, ask that the participants observe certain ground rules (no interruptions, no name calling, profanity, or physical violence), insist on the confidentiality of the proceedings by everyone present, and, in the case of social service agencies, inform participants that hints of child, adult, or self-abuse will have to be reported to appropriate agencies. Mediators reaffirm that participants are present voluntarily and are willing to try to find a solution. They congratulate the participants on their willingness to try mediation.

2. **Uninterrupted Time:** Each participant is invited to describe for the mediators his or her perspective of the conflict. Mediators encourage participants to share feelings as well as facts. Mediators may interrupt to paraphrase or clarify but the

other participant may not speak while the other person is talking. At the end of the two presentations mediators meet privately to list the important issues that have emerged and to organize the rest of the mediation around those issues. Mediators may also invite each disputant for a short, private meeting to discover if there are any other points or feelings that need to be aired. Confidentiality of this session is also assured. The mediators are at this point adequately informed about the dispute and the participants have put their thoughts and feelings into words.

3. **Exchange:** Using I-messages, participants are directed to face each other and each speaks in turn saying what happened and how he or she feels about the events. After a few sentences the other person paraphrases or summarizes what has just been said. The speaker is encouraged to comment on the accuracy of the summary. This stage of the mediation allows each party to "walk in the shoes" of the other person.

4. **Solution:** Participants are encouraged to brainstorm solutions. Suggestions are not judged for feasibility but are offered at random by the participants. By asking participants to respond to the workability of suggested solutions, mediators assist the thinking of the disputants to become practical.

5. **Agreement:** Mediators sense when participants are reaching closure and test the solutions that appear to be favored by asking each party if the solutions work for them. A document listing solutions including specific details about compliance is prepared, and each mediator and participant signs and receives a copy.

6. **Conclusion:** Mediators compliment participants for their hard work and remind them of the confidentiality of the proceedings and the agreement.

Philosophic Assumptions

The process described above rests on several philosophic assumptions:

1. Participants are responsible for devising their own solutions to the conflict. The mediator will not suggest alternatives because only the participants are able to discover solutions that are best for them. That the actions agreed to in the agreement will be followed is much more likely when the participants come up with the solutions themselves.

2. The mediator's neutrality promotes a level playing field between the participants. An imbalance of power will diminish the possibility of reaching a solution that is satisfactory to both parties.

3. Mediators operate on the knowledge that beliefs held by participants cannot be mediated; only behaviors are mediatable.

By the structure of its process and by its philosophy, mediation empowers individuals and thus provides a mechanism for personal growth. Its efficacy is attested to by the growing number of profit and not-for-profit programs that have come into existence in the United States.

Peer Mediation

An important focus of the mediation process has been the peer mediation program in public schools. Each time major violence has occurred in a public school hindsight has suggested that a peer mediation program might have identified the underlying conflict and possibly could have avoided the resulting tragedy. Utilizing students to mediate student conflicts, peer mediation has proved effective in grades four through twelve. Schools report significant decrease in violence as a direct and dramatic result of peer conflict management efforts.

In some schools students wear t-shirts identifying them as conflict managers. When a dispute occurs, school authorities offer two choices: participate in peer mediation or go to the principal. Peer mediation is usually the choice. Conducted by trained students of the same grade level as the disputants in the presence of a school counselor, the dispute is likely to be solved quickly and effectively in most cases. As with adults, mediators and participants involved learn important skills in communication and problem solving.

Restorative Justice

One important expression of the mediation movement is the concept of restorative justice. It provides a new approach to understanding and responding to crime and victimization. It encourages greater involvement of crime victims and community members in achieving justice through direct interaction with offenders. Offenders are thus held directly accountable to the people and communities they have violated. They are confronted with the emotional and material losses of victims. Victims and offenders are given opportunities for dialogue, negotiation, and problem solving, thus revealing motivations for the offense, providing information about the crime, and discussing appropriate restitution. Outcomes have included closure for the victim and a sense of renewed security, and for the offender, empathy for the victim and a sense of accountability. The outcome of such interventions is not "soft on crime" but requires more responsible behavior on the part of the offender, who must make appropriate restitution to the victim in addition to or instead of the less-than-direct correctional punishment.

Currently a number of research projects studying the mechanisms and forces at work in mediation are under way in Canada, Australia, and New Zealand, as well as in the United States. Although studies are not yet extensive or complete, early findings suggest several interesting effects of restorative justice. In dealing with crimes such as theft, minor battery, vandalism, burglary, and property defacement, restorative justice mediation has reduced the likelihood of repeat offenses. Less vindictive than expected, communities informed of its potential appear to be concerned with holding offenders accountable while being quite supportive of community-based sanctions that allow for more restorative outcomes.

In more than a thousand communities in North America and Europe, formal organizations such as Victim Offender Reconciliation Programs (VORP) or Victim-Offender Mediation (VOM) provide opportunities for victims to meet their offenders face-to-face, talk directly about the impact of the crime on their lives, express their concerns, and work out restitution. Of the impact of restorative justice, Mark Umbreit of the Center for Restorative Justice and Mediation at the University of Minnesota has written: "Juvenile offenders seem to perceive victim-offender mediation as an equally demanding response to their criminal behavior than other options available to the court. The use of mediation is consistent with the concern to hold young offenders accountable for their criminal behavior" (1994:154).

The Future

The call for formal mediation has grown tremendously in the United States and abroad. Its sphere of influence has extended to include a broad range of disputes—between persons, within families, and in educational, occupational, medical, governmental, ethnic, international, and environmental situations. The challenge for the future to this promising alternative to traditional judicial methods is fivefold: more education about the advantages of mediation needs to be available to the public; more research needs to be conducted in order to refine mediation's techniques; mediation needs to be incorporated into institutional practices; a standard certification needs to be created and canons of ethics developed; and funding for mediation services needs to be more widespread. Toward these objectives, the Society of Professionals in Dispute Resolution (SPIDR) was established in 1973.

With the creation of an office of conflict resolution, the RLDS Church has recognized the promise of mediation and responded to the scriptural call to take leadership in resolving conflict with peace and justice. The potential for resolving conflict in constructive ways within the church itself and for influencing the communities in which trained members live is immense. Church members now have a new and important asset in their pursuit of peace.

For Reflection and Discussion

1. How do you agree or disagree with the selection of the feminist movement, the Harvard Program on Negotiation, and the work of Covey and Peck as influences toward a "kinder and gentler" American society? What other influences would you add?

2. Discuss how these movements might correlate to the RLDS Church's mission and emphasis on peace, reconciliation, and healing of the spirit.

3. List and discuss sections of the Doctrine and Covenants that have been foundational to the present focus of the church on peace. Discuss the context of each of these.

4. If you have had experience in a judicial system as a jurist or in another role, or have been involved in a mediation or restorative justice situation, tell what it was like and how well you felt justice was accomplished. What would have made the experience and outcome better?

5. What would be the advantages of using alternative dispute resolution methods rather than the traditional legal system?

6. Mediators must receive training to be qualified to lead a mediation. Find out what training is available by contacting the Conflict Resolution specialist at the World Church Offices.

Sources Consulted

Ellen Berg, "Gendering Conflict Resolution," *Peace & Change* 19, no. 4 (October 1994): 325–348.

Robert A. Bush and Joseph Folger, *The Promise of Mediation* (San Francisco: Jossey-Bass, 1994).

Stephen R. Covey, *The 7 Habits of Highly Effective People* (New York: Simon & Schuster, 1989).

Roger Fisher and William Ury, *Getting to Yes* (New York: Hougton Mifflin, 1981).

Joseph Folger, Marshall Poole, Randall Stutman, *Working through Conflict* (Reading, Massachusetts: Addison-Wesley Educational Publishers, 1997).

Charles McCollough, *Resolving Conflict with Justice and Peace* (Cleveland, Ohio: Pilgrim Press, 1991).

Christopher Moore, *The Mediation Process* (San Francisco: Jossey-Bass, 1996).

M. Scott Peck, *The Road Less Traveled* (New York: Simon & Schuster, 1978).

Mark Umbreit, *Crime and Reconciliation* (Nashville, Tennessee: Abingdon Press, 1985).

Mark Umbreit, *Victim Meets Offender* (Monsey, New York: Willow Tree Press, 1994).

Chapter Five

Germany: The Wall Came Down

By Kerstin Jeske Kristiansen and Eva Erickson

Introduction

East Germany was closed off from the Western world with the building of the Berlin Wall in 1961. Religion and church activities at times were not permitted or at least not favored. In 1989 the wall came down and a year later Germany officially became one again. Naturally, we will write about the "peaceful revolution" in 1989, but we will also include some experiences and activities from before that. We shall begin with a short history of the peace movement in Germany.

The German Peace Movement

German history is complex and has, unfortunately, not been the most peaceful. We won't even attempt to analyze the involvement of German people in bringing about any war. We want to raise awareness of the fact that there are and always have been German people being active for peace.

In 1795 Immanuel Kant wrote the publication, *Zum Ewigen Frieden (To Eternal Peace)*, in which he laid some theoretical ground rules for people's rights and international peace. It was not until almost a hundred years later, in 1892, that the *Deutsche Friedensgesellschaft* (German Peace Society) was established in Berlin by the publisher Alfred Hermann Fried. An important event helping the establishment of the German Peace Society was the publication of the novel *Die Waffen Nieder! (Down the Weapons!)* by Baroness Bertha von Suttner. As a successful journalist and author, she was an activist and traveled internationally to preach her vision of a conflict-free world. In 1905 she became the first woman to receive the Nobel Peace Prize. She died just before the First World War began in 1914. By that time, about 10,000 pacifists were organized in the German peace movement. Carl von Ossietzky identified one of the reasons for the setback, saying that the peace movement was based on the "....novel of a very sensitive and very starry-eyed woman. With due deference to the extraordinary and pure wanting of Suttner, she didn't find any stronger way of expressing her ideas than to feel sorry. She was fighting with holy water against cannons...." [1]

Military and civil authorities put an end to any organized attempts of pacifistic activities in 1914, which made the German peace movement at that time basically a series of single fates. The resurrection came in 1918 and, by 1927, the German Peace Society counted about 30,000 members. [2]

For several years after the war, various peace-supporting organizations held demonstrations against war on August 1, the anniversary of the outbreak of World War I. In 1921, there were almost 200,000 people on the streets of Berlin alone. However, in the late twenties the peace movement was paralyzed by the conflict of concepts and organizational questions. Liberal and radical ideas were clashing and, by 1928, there were twenty-seven organizations that were part of the German Peace Cartel. [3]

Representatives of pacifism based on religious roots have been active since the beginnings of the peace movement. They, too, began to form several of their own peace unions—according to their different denominations—after World War I. Active pacifism in Germany included all variations at that time, from individual conscientious objection to Gandhi's teachings about nonviolence.

Another literary work of importance against the war was the novel *Im Westen Nichts Neues (All Quiet on the Western Front)* by Erich-Maria Remarque in 1929. This novel became the most important and influential anti-war book (because it was authentic) and a whole generation recognized themselves in it. Of course, it didn't take long before the government prohibited the book and the film, which came out one year later.[4] After the takeover of the government by Adolf Hitler, the pacifistic literature was forbidden and most of it was burned in 1933.

We certainly realize that the German peace movement has not been very successful. However, it is good to remember that there have always been people who tried to make their voice known and fought for peace. Today's peace movement is exclusively protesting against acute threats. One example would be the revival of the movement in the 1980s at the time of the NATO-Start II program, where hundreds of thousands demonstrated against further armament in all big cities in the western part of Germany. However, the peace movement certainly isn't one of the strongest movements in Germany.

The disaster of World Wars I and II make people want to believe this can't happen again, but most people are rarely engaged in any activities for peace. The young people, and especially the students, have almost always been at the forefront in the cause of peace. They are the ones trying to raise awareness and are ready to take any risk. The current war (March 1999) in the former country of Yugoslavia makes people suddenly realize how fragile peace really is. There is war again in Europe! Hopefully this will help people understand that peace doesn't just "happen."

Peace Issues in East Germany

In East Germany the word "peace" was used surprisingly often. The leading party, the SED (Socialist Unity Party of Germany), had peace initiatives as part of its party programs, and children learned songs like "*Kleine Weisse Friedenstaube*" ("Little White Peace Dove") in elementary school. September 1 was observed in all schools as International Day of Peace through special activities and sometimes public demonstrations for peace. However, the meaning of peace for the SED was different than it sounded. It was mostly an excuse for defense spending and armament against NATO (North Atlantic Treaty Organization). As a matter of fact, the SED initiated a collection of signatures by the general public for a "Declaration of Peace." The content of this declaration was to support the "peace initiatives" of the Soviet Union and to speak against the deployment of NATO arms in West Germany and western Europe. It was only in church settings that people were able to talk publicly about pacifism. The government saw pacifism as a threat to its politics. It appears that the church was frequently used to voice opinions regarding issues like pacifism or to make political statements. It was the only relatively safe place to do so.

Military Service

In East Germany it was mandatory for young men to do at least one and a half years of military service and three years if they wanted to go to university. Young men refusing to perform military service could expect to be sent to prison.

Today things are a little different. Young men objecting to military service do not have to go to prison but can opt to do civil service instead. In recent years the number of conscientious objectors to military service has risen higher than ever. Even though the mandatory military service time is only ten months, more and more young men choose to do the thirteen months of civil service instead. According to German law, no one can be forced into military service with a weapon against his conscience. In 1998 the number of conscientious objectors reached a new record. Since 1991 there have been more than 100,000 men annually objecting to military service. The main reason given is that military service doesn't seem "trendy" any longer, rather than a rejection to the military in general. Many people think that since the fall of the Berlin Wall and the reunification of Germany there aren't any direct threats to peace anymore![5]

Church and Peace

The Protestant Church in East Germany, and especially the youth movement of that church, called "Junge Gemeinde" (Young Congregation), was the initiator of many peace activities from the beginning of the eighties on. In 1980 the Protestant Church wanted to organize an event called "Peace Week" that was supposed to take place in all parts of East Germany. There were several reasons this "Peace Week" did not happen, but out of that idea developed something called "Friedensdekade" (Peace Decade—decade meaning ten days, not ten years).

The church was looking for a general theme for the Peace Decades. The idea for a theme came from a young pastor who had had the privilege of traveling to New York. He saw the sculpture that the Soviet Union had given to the United Nations depicting a hero making swords into plowshares, along with the scripture "...they shall beat their swords into plowshares, and their spears into pruning hooks..." (Micah 4:3). And so the theme became "Swords into Plowshares." In addition to the general theme, each of the Peace Decades had its own theme.

The first Peace Decade took place in 1980 under the theme "Make Peace without Weapons." There were a surprisingly high number of local congregations taking part in this event. Eva remembers that her own Protestant congregation in Brandenburg had an event organized with workshops, peace worships, peace prayers, song festivals, and other activities.

At first, the government had no problem with the Peace Decades or the theme and symbol. As a matter of fact, there was a governmental youth activity with the theme "Make Peace without NATO weapons," clearly imitating the popular church activity! However, when young people started displaying the symbol of the Peace Decades, for instance on their coats, the government prohibited that. They claimed the wearing of the symbol publicly was aimed against the official peace policy. Once again, within the church it was okay to voice your opinion regarding peace and against any weapons, but publicly it was seen as a threat to the government.[6]

The Peaceful Revolution

With the first Peace Decade in 1980, another new tradition, the Peace Prayers, began. These prayers took place every Monday night at 5:00 p.m. at a prominent church in Leipzig. In the beginning, the prayers were very nonpolitical. However, in 1989 things changed. The situation in East Germany was getting difficult. The Berlin Wall was erected in 1961 to keep out "the enemy," but in reality kept in all the people who were trying to leave the eastern part of Germany. It was not allowed to travel to the West or even to visit relatives in West Germany, except for pensioners and, in rare cases, people with special permission. However, it was allowed for West Germans to come to East Germany. Many people were dissatisfied with this situation.

From 1986 on it began getting easier to leave the East in order to visit relatives in the West and to obtain special permissions, for business conferences or even international church events. One example is Kerstin's father, who was able to represent the East Germany Church at the RLDS World Conference in the United States. Another example is two friends of ours who were allowed to attend an international youth retreat in Norway in 1988. With more people being able to travel and experience the "Western world," dissatisfaction with the totalitarian system in East Germany grew, and people became increasingly outspoken.

In May 1989 Hungary became the first country from the Eastern Bloc to open its borders to the West. It wasn't difficult for East Germans to travel to Hungary, which meant that many, especially young people, went there for vacation during that summer and never returned. Following that, many other people went to the West German embassies in Prague and Warsaw to do the same.

The situation within the country became very tense. The church warned against "extreme actions and demonstrations" as "no means of the church" but demanded from the government free elections, the right to demonstrate, and a variety of political parties.[7] Different political groups formed and asked for democratic reforms. The peace prayers, still held every Monday at 5:00 p.m., changed dramatically. Demonstrations were held after the prayer, and the voices became loud and clear. Soon the prayers, as well as the demonstrations, spread to other cities and attracted more and more people.

The East German government decided to celebrate its fortieth anniversary on October 7, despite all the uproar. Thousands dared to protest against the regime and there were many incidences with the police. Church leaders used their government connections and the trust of the people to urge nonviolence. On Monday night, October 9, 70,000 people demonstrated in Leipzig, as well as more people at various other places. It was the first demonstration with slogans like "We are the people" and "No violence." The atmosphere was tense; people hadn't forgotten that the SED had applauded the bloody suppression of the student demonstration in China only a few months before. Police and army were on the alert, and an order to shoot at the demonstrators had been given. Why, in the end, things worked out peacefully has never been totally clear. Apparently, there was some confusion and misunderstanding among the police force and their superiors. And, after all, the people were not doing anything but praying and marching on the streets with candles in their hands. Nonviolence was a key to success.

One month later the wall was unexpectedly opened and, within less than a year, Germany was one country again. All these events became known as "The Peaceful Revolution." The churches had been a vital force in urging nonviolence during that time. They are still active, unfortunately with much lower attendance. The net of the secret police had been incredibly tight and no one was sure whom to trust. Feelings of betrayal, hatred, and anger were directed to anyone involved, but the churches tried to bring peace again and asked everyone to forgive and reconcile. The peace prayers have continued. They are still held weekly, without demonstrations, "open to everyone."

Today, the East Side Gallery is a witness of the time "behind the Iron Curtain." The East Side Gallery is part of the former wall in Berlin. It's about a mile long and stands between the underground stations "Hauptbahnhof" and "Warschauer Strasse." Many artists from all over the world have used their talents and creativity to paint this gallery and to express their dreams and wishes. Many of the pictures are devoted to peace issues.

For Reflection and Discussion

1. How strong has the peace movement been in your country? At what time was it the strongest and why?

2. When have you seen the word "peace" applied to something other than peace-centered objects or activities?

3. What are the laws in your country about being a conscientious objector? What official stand has the RLDS Church taken on the issue? (See World Conference Resolutions 1061, 1087, 1129, and 1249. To read these see Rules and Resolutions (1990) and supplements, available from Herald House.)

4. What effect do you think the ministry of the churches had on the unification of Germany? Have the churches played a role in peaceful revolutions in other countries or situations? What does this tell us?

5. What insights did you gain from this chapter? What have you understood more clearly by looking at peace through German eyes?

Notes

1. W. Benz, *Von Bertha von Suttner bis Carl von Ossietzky: Die deutsche Friedensbewegung 1890–1939* (Frankfurt am Main: Fischer Taschenbuch Verlag, 1998).
2. F. K. Scheer, *Die Deutsche Friedensgesellschaft (1892–1933). Organisation, Ideologie, politische Ziele. Ein Beitraf zur Geschichte des Pazifismus in Deutschland* (Frankfurt, 1981).
3. R. Lutgemeier-Davin, *Pazifismus zwischen Kooperation und Konfrontation. Das Deutsche Friedenskartell in der Weimarer Republik* (Koln, 1982).
4. Benz.
5. *Frankfurter Neue Presse*, 13.01.99 *http://www.dfg-vk.de/Zivildienst/zahl005.htm.*
6. F. Dorgerloh, *Geschichte der Evangelischen Jugendarbeit in der DDR. Teil 1*, A.J. Edition. (Missionshandlung Hermannsburger Verlagsgesellschaft) 1999.
7. C. Schulzki-Haddouti. *Kirchenpolitik in der DDR;* (1990); *http://members.aol.com/infowelt/frau.html.*

Chapter Six

Nigeria: Peace Is a Process Like Gardening

By Joseph Charlie

Introduction to the Country

Nigeria is the most populous black nation of the world. With a population of approximately 120 million, it has more than 250 unique ethnic groups and more than a thousand languages and dialects. Nigeria is a complex linguistic, social, and cultural mosaic. The Hausa and Fulani people occupy the northern part of the country. The Yoruba and the Ibo occupy the southwest and southeast respectively. Other tribes include the Edo, Ijaw, Annang, and Ibibio of the south; the Nupe, Tiv, and Kanuri of the central and northeastern parts of the country.

Nigeria is also religiously diverse. About 48 percent of the population is Muslim while 38 percent are Christians, with Roman Catholicism, Methodism, Pentecostalism, and Evangelicalism being the most influential. The remainder of the population practices other traditional religions.

Nigeria has a long and rich tradition of arts, with literature, religious paraphernalia, rituals, and other arts dating as far back as 500 B.C.E. Some of them include the terra-cotta Ife, terra-cottas, and Benin bronze work first made around A.D. 1200. Nigerian culture has a long tradition of oral literature passed down from generation to generation. Each ethnic group has folktales, legends, sayings, symbols, stories, and beliefs about peace—each different from another. I will attempt to share the concept of peace in general between these tribes and will use tribal illustrations and stories to support my information. I will also draw from a wealth of personal experience from my Annang tribe.

What Does Your Culture Say about Peace?

With more than 250 ethnic groups and languages spoken there, Nigeria encompasses a vast cultural diversity. We are shaped largely by cultures that have been handed down to us through learned languages and symbols. Thus the intellectual, moral, and spiritual wisdom gained by our forebears is preserved in our culture. In many Nigerian cultures, self-expression is frowned upon, dialogue is discouraged, and people are not confronted assertively and directly, because to do so is considered rude and arrogant. Creating an environment promoting peace helps people see eye to eye.

Nigeria, like many other African countries, is a paternalistic society. Therefore, understanding and working through gender issues is needed to frame peaceful interaction. Disagreements are resolved through avoidance or accommodation. As a result, considerable effort is given to face-saving. Cultural considerations include attention to the place of nonverbal communication, time, relationship, and face-saving.

All of us would like the world to be better, even though we may not agree on just how bad it is or exactly what remedies are appropriate, but we know that many people get a raw deal. Peace is an indescribable feeling that one has after an action or event. It is associated with joy, well-being, unity, obedience, contentment, hope, and love. It is also connected with security. It can be set in contrast to disorder. Peace is being whole and complete, all things pulling together for good in life in its comprehensive sense—including eating, health, fellowship, and hope.

The Annang culture believes in settling disputes amicably. In the pre-Christian era, the gods of the land were appeased annually by sacrifices, pouring libations, and other traditional practices for peace in the land. Some of the men have worn white clay marks on their faces and necks as a symbol of surrender and search for peace. Today, our culture has undergone transformation and modification. In place of sacrifices and other practices, people meet to pray and connect their faith with daily living. They meet with elders of the community to settle boundary and family disputes. With the help of parents and church ministers, marital conflicts are settled. Peace becomes a necessity for living.

What Do the Stories, Legends, Folk Tales, Sayings, and Symbols Say about Peace?

A country as diverse as Nigeria has numerous sayings and tales about peace. Peace to the Annang people is found within and must be cultivated and nurtured. The Annang people are mostly farmers and see peace as a garden where every vegetable needed for daily use is planted. The bush is cleared and burned, signifying a need for people to have an open mind and to rid their minds of anything that may hamper peace. Then the ground is tilled and seeds are planted for future growth. Because many people practice subsistence farming, different varieties of seed are planted together. Farm work is unending with unwanted weeds to be pulled and watering by the farmer when rain is inadequate. Sunlight is needed for the plants to grow. The more care given the garden, the more fruitful the outcome. The yams need stakes and careful tending so the stem does not climb the wrong stake. The corn needs space. So do the pumpkin leaves, the cassava, the water yam, the melon, the green pepper. These all compete among each other for space.

When the corn is harvested, the yams have room to grow until harvest. The truth undergirding this story is that peace is something you must continue to work on—a lifelong process just like gardening.

There is a story about the goshawk. This bird was hungry and decided to go with his wife looking for food. They saw smoke and fire and some dead snails, flies, and locusts underneath as they hovered in the sky. Eventually the female goshawk decided to go closer to the smoke and pick some food to take home while the male goshawk was to watch out for her. A quarrel ensued between the female hawk and the smoke. The female goshawk accused the smoke of blocking her view of the food and her husband. The smoke accused the female goshawk of invading her privacy. The female goshawk ended up blind and was consumed by fire, while the male returned without the female or food. From that time on, whenever a bush is burned and the smoke climbs high, the male goshawk will always visit the scene, crying and whistling for the wife to hear him and return.

There is a link with this story to our hope for peace. Whenever there is a dispute (smoke), we may be so blinded that we go back to our previous state of mind. Our eyes may be smoke-filled and our heart suffocated. Sometimes we lose our senses to the smoke and do not return. We may even use harmful objects in attempts to clear our eyes and hearts. Religious experiences bring reconciliation and healing when we use the right tools. We sing our sorrows away and oftentimes look to the sky to ask God to take over. We always sing new tunes to bring about peace. There will always be smoke, yet we have to be in the forefront for peace.

There is another legendary story, which is perhaps the most intriguing of all. All villages were invited by the god of the land to come and receive what they lacked and get their needs met. The village town crier announced that all its citizens should take large containers like basins, cans, or trucks to the meeting. Many took basins, expecting to take home in large quantity whatever was offered to them for the village. Many villages defied the order and took baskets, small basins, or hoes, saying, "I do not have to labor myself too hard on behalf of the village. If I am asked to work, I will be very careful and would work lazily with my small hoe and unsharpened machetes." When the giver came out, she noticed giant basins and large water containers and decided to give all villages water that day. The roll was called and every village that brought basins and giant water containers got enough water for the whole village. Those villagers who brought hoes and baskets were disappointed that their container could not hold water. When every village had taken its share, the giver then left.

The villagers returned to their respective villages to report to the elders what they received from the giver on behalf of the village. Many of the villagers were very disappointed and angry that they did not have containers to bring water to the village and, as a result, the villagers decided to go to the other villages and steal their water. The villages with water fought to keep their gift because the people thought their gift of water would be exhausted, while the villages without water decided to open a market and stop the villagers with water from coming to buy from their market. After a long period of fighting and disputes, the giver summoned all the villages again and blessed all of them abundantly. Those villages with water would have it in abundance, and those with land would have it in abundance, and those with the market would have abundant fruit to sell and so on. Thus, there was peace in the land because everyone shared their gifts with each other.

Peace requires giving back the gifts received from the giver. I am a member of the Rotary club and the four-way test of the things we think, say, or do is this: (1) Is it the truth? (2) Is it fair? (3) Will it be beneficial to all concerned? (4) Will it bring goodwill and better friendships? These principles can be applied to govern our lives secularly and religiously.

Has Peace Been More Important in Some Time Periods Than Others?

Naturally, peace will be more important during civil, religious, and tribal war, political instability, or boundary disputes. Many African countries have suffered these crises, perhaps more than countries in the West. We have heard of the disputes and warring factions in Liberia, Sierra Leone, Angola, South Africa, and Democratic Republic of the Congo, just to mention a few. Nigeria went through a period of civil war for three years from 1967–1970. Nigeria, like any country facing similar situations, was damaged physically and her citizens psychologically, socially, and politically. There was divisiveness throughout the four regions of the country, each accusing the other of betrayal. To stop the incessant killings and untold hardship, reaching a peaceful settlement was much more important than seeking who was right and who was wrong. It took courageous leadership to bring reconciliation to the warring regions.

But I believe peace is important at all times. It is necessary to preserve the cordial coexistence socially, politically, and religiously as long as we breathe.

How Have History and Geography Affected Your Country's View of Peace?

History and geography have a negative effect on Nigeria's concept of peace. Histories of political oppression in certain geographical areas continue to divide the country in all aspects of life. The northern part is predominantly Muslim and their religious beliefs and practices affect their concept of peace. The south and southeast regions are predominantly Christian, and their understanding of peace is also affected by their religious beliefs and practices. Our approach toward peace among tribes and ethnic groups is made more difficult by unfounded historical events as told by the elderly, creating a divisive mentality among these groups of people.

Is Interest in Peace Growing or Declining?

Interest in peace is on the rise because it is a necessity for living. However, there are varied strategies. Because of the pluralistic, religious, economic, and political nature of Nigeria, approaches to peace have witnessed a combination of force and power (as in the 1967 civil war), military dictatorship, jihad, conflict resolution, local unwritten customs and rites, individual and organizational efforts, arbitration, and prayers. Unlike the past, the government now has arbitration committees, boundary dispute committees, reconciliation teams, and such in villages, and on the local and state level.

What Values in Your Culture Support Peace?

Intertribal marriages have helped in bridging the tribal gaps that long existed. Communal clashes have decreased because of the taboo of having any malicious thoughts on in-laws and grandchildren. Grandchildren belong to the community. In this value, peace is the reconciliation that children and grandchildren bring between tribes that are normally antagonistic to each other. It is also a restoration of right relationships between God and the people—a relationship of interdependence. This value reminds me of the church seal—the lion, the lamb, and little child. What would the world be without children?

Hospitality as a value supports peace in my culture. Every guest in our homes will be treated to a fish and pepper-sauce dish. The sauce is made from palm oil and pepper. The guest will partake of this meal with an open and clean heart—without recourse. Conversation will only begin after the meal. Therefore a covenant of peace, a relationship that restores everlasting wholeness, is entered. In other surrounding cultures, guests will be given a cup of water to signify peaceful coexistence.

Eating together was one of the principal hallmarks of Jesus' ministry. Most often, Jesus would refer to eating together as a sign of peace, where all can sit down together irrespective of cultural, religious, economic, and political status and the poor will have enough to eat. Therefore peace and food come together in promoting community.

Has Christianity or the Restoration Movement Had Any Effect on the Culture in Regard to Peace?

There are biblical accounts of Jesus gathering the wretched, the sick, and the poor of the village to form a community of solidarity in which people helped each other. Through this action, Jesus and his followers carried peace throughout the land, the peace of the kingdom of God, which one could already see, touch, smell, and taste. As a Christian, I believe Christian doctrines and beliefs have impacted my concept of peace. I think a Muslim will give the same answer if asked. Previously, the cultures of Nigeria and the geographical divide would affect my approach to answering this question. I am thankful that our church was founded with the peace emphasis in mind. My exposure to cultures of the West has significantly reduced my geographical bias toward violence.

I spent about five years in the United States studying at Park College. I was surprised to receive a call from a Nigerian that I did not know. He invited me to a meeting of Nigerians in Kansas City. I arrived at the meeting without many expectations. There were Nigerians from all tribes in Nigeria eating, sharing, laughing together, a situation that is eluding those in Nigeria. I left the meeting energized and changed. I deemphasized tribes and regional divide from my "mainframe" and injected Restoration principles.

Our history as a denomination reminds us that there were times when our conflict-resolution approach was militant, resulting in many people losing their lives and resources. But over and over again, we are drawn to the purpose to which we were and still are being called—to build Zion. Zion is to be a community of solidarity where people help each other—just like Jesus taught. Because we can imagine the future, we are not limited to our immediate sensory experience. Because I imagine the benefits of being in a better shape and fitness for soccer, I can continue my training exercise in the gym, on the practice pitch, despite the sensory discomfort it oftentimes immediately brings. I would be foolish to ignore the critical role the physical world plays in achieving my desire for better physical soccer fitness. I believe we cannot truly claim peace if we do not work at it and imagine the benefits.

Throughout history, communities where the Restoration gospel and message were present have witnessed of new life-transforming experiences. Our belief in the worth of persons and liberty of conscience has given communities cause to work together for good, irrespective of their religious affiliations. Ikot Oku Mfang, my community, is one of these. The church is the life of the community. Because of this our culture has witnessed gradual transformation. Interestingly, our vision to become a worldwide church dedicated to the pursuit of peace, reconciliation, and healing of the spirit reminded us of our founding focus.

Restoration principles and doctrines have touched only about 10,000 people in just four of the thirty-six states of the Nigerian federation. It is therefore accurate to say that though small in number, members and friends of the church through their daily Christian living have been affected by the Restoration doctrine.

For many years my village spent hundreds of thousands of Naira (the national currency) over a boundary dispute with a neighboring village. Many lives and properties were lost in both villages. One year our neighboring village asked all its inhabitants to stay away from our village, although no one from that village can get to the city without passing through Ikot Oku Mfang. Many of their wards are students in the Saints Comprehensive Secondary School, my village school. When Sunday Charlie Akpan heard of their resolve, he went to the school to announce that he would bus students back and forth between the two villages and invited the many people to support his action. Many people claim that my village is at peace today because of such practical Restoration principles. We now live in peace, and resources are tailored to better the economic and structural features of the village.

What Aspects of Your Culture Illuminate the Gospel?

The world is full of abundant resources yet lacking in human attention. When I was growing up in the village of Ikot Oku Mfang, our community-style living, where each and everyone cares and shares with each other, remained a primary example of Zionic living. Many times I remember a neighbor coming to our house to ask for salt or oil because she ran out and my mom generously gave to her. It is also common to see food criss-crossing to and from homes, especially in the evenings. Whether your mom cooked that evening or not, every household would have a choice of three or more meals to choose from. Community (Zionic) living, sharing, caring, and hospitality are the aspects of my culture that have remained.

Our cultural belief that everyone is capable aligns well with our church's teachings on the worth of persons. No child should be thrown away, because she or he may turn out to be the leader the community wants. Respect for all persons in the community illuminates the gospel. Our belief in the transcendent and the hope that tomorrow will be better than today economically, religiously, and otherwise is an expression of hope and faith.

How Does the Gospel Make You Critical of Your Culture?

Our culture is undergoing pluralistic transformation because of the influence of cultures of surrounding countries. However, many governments still practice instant justice—tit for tat—and this is in contrast with the religious teachings. The government still executes prisoners and people it considers nonsupportive of government policies. But perhaps the aspect of my culture to be most criticized is patriarchy.

I struck up a conversation with a Hausa man—who is also a Muslim—about what he understands to be peace and the principles of life that will promote peaceful living. His reply was interwoven with his culture and religion. He values his wife and believes that any man who approaches his wife without permission is not promoting peaceful living. He also said that it is religiously appropriate to eliminate any person who does not promote peace and unity. Peace to him is linked with material and economic satisfaction: Whether he can feed his family and provide his wife with everything she needs to prevent any other man from seeing her outside. He believes women cause most of the disputes and so they should be isolated. His culture dictates that women be isolated—not even her parents or relatives can see her. He acknowledged that both the Quran and Bible have similar notions about peace and unity. His only exception is that many Christian denominations are not practicing what they preach.

I was awed to hear that women cause most of the disputes. The biblical accounts of the most peaceful and caring people include women and I do not agree with the notion of isolation. Like the story shared previously, everyone has a gift to share in the building of a peaceful kingdom. His last statement struck me as well. If we will practice what we preach and live the difference, we can join hands with other cultures and religions to promote healthy and peaceful living.

There are women with endless experiences of domination by men in the African culture. One central fact that must be faced is that men are frequently the source of violence that tears down families, communities, and even nations. My culture accounts for this by noting that men are more aggressive physically than are females, and that this goes back to our distant past when the man's strength was needed to defend women. Yet women are the ones left to find alternative ways of repairing the damage that men's violence and conflict have wrought. They are the survivors when the men are no longer there, forcing them to find alternatives that break the deadlock of a conflictive situation. They are the ones who find nonviolent ways in a potentially violent situation. They teach others how to cope, to heal memories, to move on. Gender equality is an aspect of equal rights and a major player toward peace, but so far it has remained a very little-acknowledged prerequisite of peace.

Indeed, so much have aggression and conflict come to characterize our social, economic, and religious systems that many have come to believe that such behavior is intrinsic to human nature and impossible to eliminate. The gospel calls us to peacemaking, not by directing our thinking along these traditional power channels, but by making possible the springing of alternatives to dominative power. To counter power with the same kind of power, I believe, does not lead to peace. Peace requires finding a different kind of power from dominative power to transform situations. Perhaps peace is not something we can anticipate. However, anticipating peace can be a way of disciplining our quest and keeping us focused on the ultimate goal, and it may prepare us if and when peace finally does arrive. Peace is also attributed as a feeling of fulfillment and joy, yet surprise, puzzlement, and even confusion can grip us when peace occurs.

What Have Been Some of Your Struggles between Gospel and Culture?

The introduction of the gospel has brought mixed blessings to our people. Perhaps we were not allowed to express our theology in ways it could fit with the gospel. Our cultures have struggled with which parts of the traditional societies and superstitions to keep and which to let go. In the olden days, there were traditional societies that unified the people for a common purpose—love. These societies had their beliefs and rituals. They paraded as masqueraders in the daytime and met late at night. They had meals together, celebrated each other's progress, and mourned with bereaved members.

These societies and their beliefs formed the foundation that made Christianity easily adopted but with modifications. Instead of sacrifices and other rituals, we embrace the love of Christ as the only sacrifice.

We are a people who celebrate life. Our celebration comes in the form of music, clapping, dancing, and drumming. With singing that flows from the heart, local instruments blend to give proper rhythm. The sound of music brings a typical African to life. But we almost missed that part of our culture. The early missionaries dictated the form of music and rhythm to conform to their own kind of music. All forms of instrumentation were discouraged. Our joy, an aspect of life that transcended our poor economic and social situation, was belittled with comments that not all forms of music are in relation to the Holy Spirit. True as that may be, they were killing the aspect of life that can revive people. The early missionaries were associating music and drumming with deities. Today, most of those early traditional churches stand empty because of the dearth of joy and celebration associated with music and dancing. The manner of dancing and the hysteria associated with music is now changing. I am gratified to belong to a church that honors and respects our culture's value of celebration. Perhaps celebration is one of the missing pieces in religious experiences of the West.

Personal: What Are Your Convictions about Peace and Justice? Where Do They Come from?

The scriptural accounts of peace are often perplexing yet very rich. There are accounts of nations fighting nations, with God in the lead; brothers fighting brothers, while God is silent. Some of the accounts result in bloodshed, untold hardship, disorder, and even a rebuking of God. Yet there is a peace of God that surpasses all understanding, which will guard our hearts and minds in Christ Jesus (Philippians 4:7) and such peace that the world cannot give (John 14:27). The scriptures tell us that the kind of peace the world gives does not last. But we must take the initiative. This is not to discredit our efforts toward peace, but to always ask the Holy Spirit for guidance and direction.

Throughout the history of the church, there were repeated calls and challenges to make communities peaceful. Therefore, the *pursuit* of peace is not new to us. It has been recounted to us in words and concepts and is the bedrock of our faith movement. But our vision of peace continues to be shaped by the environment in which we currently live. Nevertheless, the vision of the church founders continues. Therefore, the pursuit of peace is God's actual demand on us for this time and for all time. Thus it is not confined to the interim. It is a state in which the world is meant to be. It is the best description of what the reign of God will be like—a place of safety, justice, and truth; a place of trust, inclusion, and love; a place of joy, happiness, and well-being. "Blessed are the peacemakers" as promised in the Beatitudes in my mind means, blessed are those who continue to engage in the struggle for all living creatures, who try to bring people to the point of participating in the reconstruction of the corrupted creation and its battered relationship with God, neighbors, friends, and foes. "Blessed are the peacemakers" articulates the notion that the children of God do not give up when prospects appear hopeless. They continue to struggle against rejection and the refusal of others to know God's love in even small ways.

Being a member of this faith movement does not separate me from the world and its problems. At times I have experienced privately, publicly, and religiously that, despite all my personal efforts, I can neither make nor preserve peace. I have neighbors who disagree with me theologically and will not speak or even sit with me. There are people who refuse to associate with me because they are economically advantaged. There are people who, upon discovering my personal, conscientious, and religious efforts, will reject my peace efforts as a "show-off." Yet I am not discouraged. Being a member of this faith community therefore helps make me fit to live triumphantly and usefully. I become a co-creator and partner with God, trusting that the Holy Spirit will consist in recalling and recreating the vital truths and direction that have been heard and almost forgotten, and interpret them to us according to the contemporary needs of today's world.

We are called to proclaim Jesus Christ and promote communities of joy, hope, love, and peace. More than ever, our world needs both individual and group efforts in settling disputes between people and nations. Peace, then, can be synonymous with reconciliation. Peace is the grace of reconciliation and comes from within, manifesting through our response to the service of the Lord.

What Are Your Hopes and Commitments in the Redemption of Your People and Their Cultures?

What does it mean to experience peace after so much suffering, I often ask? Only those who have suffered, who carry memories of pain in their bodies, know how strong the yearning can be for peace and how far away peace can seem to be. Because we Africans have experienced personal pain, perhaps we are more open to new models of living than those in Western countries. Our common elements of humility and personal sacrifice lead to inside-out Christ-centered change. The peace that Jesus offers us is a peace that has known suffering and how costly it can be. I think peace is perhaps the final stage of reconciliation.

It is important to observe that some bad laws devised by humans have contributed tremendously to chaos and conflict all over the world. Good laws should take into account all the major players and should not be biased. Unfortunately, what has become obvious in most African countries and cultures is that the rich and powerful often manipulate and corrupt the law, forcing officers to favor them. Some bad cultural practices and beliefs cause similar conflicts and injustice. We need to change or, at best, challenge those structures and belief systems that cause misery to our people.

God is creating better, more peaceful, and richer communities because you and I are involved. God is calling us to work to support the mixing and contend with the challenges. We are assured that our efforts will not be vain, even when they remain without tangible results. The future now belongs to societies that organize themselves for learning to live together, utilizing the gifts Jesus Christ is passing on to them. The future belongs to societies that combine and continue to explore the nature of the mix between "religious," "secular," and "traditional" activities. We need to find ways in which doctrines and traditional taboos, prayerful commitment and political honesty, faithful and spiritual devotion and theocratic democracy, traditional and religious songs and social engagement, scriptures and civility can fuse together for the kind of peace that comes from Jesus Christ rather than as the world gives. We are commissioned to create peace in our homes, community, and our world. Whether peace is reached only after unimaginable horrors precipitated by humanity's stubbornness or is achieved by acts of consultative will is the choice of all those who inhabit the earth.

I have hope we can make a significant difference and be representatives of Jesus Christ in our villages, cities, and towns where we live and work. It is incumbent upon the church to become more involved in the process of peace, justice, and reconciliation. I am convinced that effectiveness in all peacemaking areas contributes to meeting the needs of the world community. Peacemaking in our homes and workplaces contributes to an overall atmosphere of lessened hostility, anger, and defensiveness and will lead us to becoming a worldwide church dedicated to the pursuit of peace, reconciliation, and healing of the spirit. The task is to commit ourselves to "doing" the Word, reconciled with God and having harmony within and without.

The barriers that hinder the propagation of world peace are mainly political and emotional problems such as doubts, misconceptions, prejudices, suspicions, and narrow self-interest that antagonize people from all over the world. There is no time to refer to some corporate center or societal icon to bring peace. Every one of us needs to manifest responsibility and leadership. The peace that Christ gives brings us together, not like popcorn kernels in a popper, where each one explodes on its own, nor like ice cubes in the freezer that freeze together, nor like a box of chocolates in the summer sun, all melted together. But whatever our interpretation may be, it brings us together joyfully, hopefully, lovingly, and peacefully. In my personal best, my question in all my actions will be, "Will it bring peace to the other person?"

If our church as an institution has failed or is failing, it is because we have forgotten that love comes first. If we work hard to discover and practice unconditional love again in our churches, government, homes, schools, factories, and offices, our people could be set free to make life-changing peace initiatives and set goals; with a relationship of interdependence, we can reach those goals. As we begin a new century, peace is needed more than ever. With both spirituality and strategy, the church must work with all people and organizations of goodwill to bring about the healing and transformation our shattered communities need. The church's role can be in the resources it brings to the peace process, and the active role it can play in it.

Perhaps some in the church are afraid that working together to heal a troubled world might introduce divisions into the church itself. I served as a member of the World Church Peace Committee from 1994 to 1998. In 1994 Barbara Higdon, then committee chair, gave a report of the committee's deliberations during the biennium. In that report, clarification was sought on approaches to peace. The World Conference was divided because those who served in the armed forces felt their service to the nation was not recognized as a strategy for peace. As a result, the report was rejected. I was sad but knew that the church was being careful not to cause another division—even when those divisions are likely already there but are deftly kept from coming to the surface.

Reading the October 1998 *Saints Herald* my usual way (from the back page to the front), I read with excitement Curt Heaviland's article "A Military for All Nations." I was drawn to this article because the armed forces newsletter of the RLDS Association for Ministry to Military Personnel has been renamed The Peace keeper. He wrote:

> The best use of the military, in a world that is oriented toward peace, has been to support and carry out the constructive wishes of the sponsoring government. Very few in military service anywhere today want any form of conflict. They do, however, want responsible governments to work for and to establish peace.

He went on to say the following:

> Just as the church is dedicated to the pursuit of peace, church members in the military are dedicated to preserving peace and justice and seeing that good agreements are honored in the service of the citizens.

That is the side of the armed forces I never knew, having been brought up where successive government leaders were members of the armed forces without respect for human rights and justice. Many military approaches to peace in Africa have been in sharp contrast to the mission of this church association, resulting in loss of lives, abuse, and economic and social instability. Our efforts toward peace are certainly diverse.

As we engage in this important spiritual journey, it is important to take cultural issues into account. To import another kind of peace process may not be effective without adaptation and modification. The church as an international organization has opportunities through its relief and development agencies to work for peace. Our church has Outreach International, the World Hunger Committee, and partners with other relief agencies too numerous to mention. I believe our intent to become a "worldwide church dedicated to the pursuit of peace, reconciliation, and healing of the spirit" is the best way of defining our mission in the world today.

May a new dawning of our human consciousness about possibilities of living in peace rise in my lifetime. Let us be the generation of reconciliation and peace. I therefore invite you to join in the search for peace—in your personal lives and as a family of God's children.

For Reflection and Discussion

1. Make a list of things the author says are important in peace. Then make a list of things you think are important to peace and compare the lists.

2. The author uses the garden, the story of the goshawk, and the story of the villages to tell us something about peace from his culture. What are some folktales, legends, or stories from your own culture that tell about peace?

3. Select a comment from the news that was stated by a public figure and apply the Rotary Club's four-way test. Discuss how you feel about the suggested four-way test.

4. What role does hospitality play in peacemaking?

5. What role do children play in peacemaking?

6. Discuss the value of people being able to express their worship through their own cultural patterns rather than through those imposed from outside.

7. Write about your understanding of peace in one paragraph and share it with others.

Chapter Seven

Kenya: Peace—Creating Right Order

By Mary Ooko

We all agree there is a great need for peace in the continent of Africa. But before we begin discussing how to bring peace, we are confounded by a basic problem of agreement on the meaning of peace, even though we regularly use the term in many contexts of our daily lives.

Peace, said Thomas Aquinas, is the "tranquility that flows from right order." When we put right order into the structures of our society, the tranquility that results is peace. And so we see that the right ordering that brings peace is closely connected to justice. When we put right order into our relationships at every level, beginning with the family and continuing right up to the government and the church, the calmness that comes out of this right ordering is peace. When we put right order into the dealings between clan and clan, between tribe and tribe, and between political party and political party, the tranquility that flows from that order is peace.

Peacemaking

The work of peacemaking is entrusted to all of Christ's disciples, women no less than men. The ministry and message entrusted to the disciples of Christ can be summed up simply as "the gospel of peace" (see Ephesians 6:15, Ephesians 2:17,

Acts 10:36). This peace characterizes both the messenger and his work: Peace is in the subject; it is also his work.

Making peace is an active role, an active ministry. It is not sitting idly by, waiting for something to happen or for events to take place. It is not just observing from the sidelines. It is not just talking about peace.

On the contrary, making peace is promoting the activities that will render peace possible, feasible, and practicable. Making peace is removing the obstacles that prevent peace from being realized. Making peace is bringing people together, often those who consider themselves to be opponents, adversaries, and enemies. Once they are together they can better see that they share a common humanity and have similar needs, hopes, dreams, and purposes in their life on this earth. Making peace is fostering mutual dialogue—speaking and listening to one another—with the aim of arriving at a consensus and finding mutually acceptable solutions. Making peace is the commitment to refuse to give in to violence, whether violent thoughts, words, or actions. Making peace is active nonviolence.

In most African countries, the ideals of peace, justice, liberty, democracy, and economic prosperity have been grossly undermined by perennial, political, social, and economic crises.

Attitudes and events of the past always form a part of the present in human life. For better or for worse, consciously or otherwise, the past molds and impels us. Therefore, individually and collectively, we are to some extent what we have been. Whether one's view of life and history is linear, cyclical, or an ever-expanding spiral, a bit of the present is in the past, and the future lies in both. We must be aware of our own past to participate with a clear vision in the process of changing the present and shaping the future.

Polygamy

Polygamy among the "Luos" of Kenya is a tradition of the past but even today among converted Christians in Luo land there are still those who practice polygamy. Despite the heartbreak and bitterness that children grow up with in polygamous homes, those who practice it take pride from the large homes they are able to manage. Polygamy has hindered the peace process in many homes in Luo land and in Kenya.

There is a polygamous Luo man, "Ancentus Akuku Oguela Danger," who was born in 1918; his youngest wife was born in 1978. His first child came in 1947 but his youngest child is only four months old. More than ninety times married, about forty times separated, Akuku is husband to about forty-five wives. At eighty, the patriarch (so called by his friends) is still going strong.

Akuku is often referred to as the "total man," the polygamist of polygamists. Akuku is a family name in the southern part of Nyanza in Kenya. When I was young I recall someone referring to him when talking about the man with more than a hundred wives, hundreds of children, and hundreds of grandchildren.

Akuku Danger claims that his first wife "Nyadendi" (Luo name for last wife) was married before to a younger man. After two years the man threw her out because "she could not have children." Akuku claims he gave her a child within record time. He beat all the young men to win the heart of a teenager.

Initially Akuku had ninety-four wives, but now there are only forty-five. The others left him for different reasons and four are dead. Akuku won't say how many children he has, but he has more daughters than sons. The number of daughters, he says, number more than 200, while the sons are fewer than a hundred. Grandchildren are many; he does not know the exact number. He is father to doctors, nurses, teachers, drivers, mechanics, and businessmen. He has also buried many. Some died when they were young; he hardly remembers. He has lost count of the younger children below age fifteen.

Akuku Danger married his first wife in 1938 when he was twenty-one. His marriage to many wives appears to be almost hereditary. His grandfather had forty-five wives but his father had only three. He brags of unmatched power. Akuku's wives know he is a good man because they get food, shelter, and clothes.

Akuku takes issue with people who say wives are a sign of wealth. He says that being wealthy is not having a wife, but one's wealth depends on how well you keep and bring up your family. The moment he brings in a new wife, he sets up a home for her. Most of his wives are scattered throughout his land, which covers several locations. Wives who come from the same places or are related are sometimes set up in the same compound.

Akuku says a man has to discipline his wives by beating them when they misbehave. Cases of Akuku's wives straying are rare, and he maintains a strict survey of what each of them does.

Akuku is also a devout Catholic and regularly attends Holy Mass at his nearest Catholic church. Akuku claims he has a good relationship with his priest, who is not offended by his lifestyle.

How did Akuku acquire the name "Danger"? During colonial days when the white man was still around, Akuku had eighteen wives. The white men began to fear him. They would hear of Akuku's large family and say, "That man is dangerous." They could not understand how Akuku could live with so many wives. Later, when the harem swelled, Akuku became not just dangerous but "Danger" itself.

Most of Akuku's children are married and have children, who in turn have children. His first grandchild, a daughter, was born in 1967. She is now thirty-one, with seven children, much older than her father's lastborn.

Akuku claims that sometimes his children do not know each other by name, but when they meet they feel the "Akuku" blood. The firstborn child and son of Akuku is a bitter man. Fifty-seven years old, Dande Akuku has not spoken to his father for more than thirty years. Dande claims his father does not visit him because a witch doctor once told him that if he does, his wealth would disappear. Dande is not happy with his father's position. He sympathizes with all the women that his father may have messed up in the process of polygamy. As a man, his father is seen as being good and superior to marry all those many women, but Dande feels it is wrong.

84

The fourth-born son, Sospeter, thinks differently of his father. He idolizes the patriarch and claims his father taught him that the cure for a jealous wife is to add another wife. Then the former wife will cool down. Sospeter says that when his first wife grew big-headed, he brought in a second one, and when she also did the same he brought in a third one. When the last two formed an alliance, thus leaving the first wife out, she had nowhere to run except back to him. When the other two saw this they had no alternative but to compete for Sospeter's attention. He claims to enjoy the competition.

Polygamy flourished in the past among the Luos of Kenya because children were viewed as a sign of wealth. Child labor in the fields was the order of the day, so children provided cheap labor. Girls were appreciated simply because of the fact that, when they got married, a dowry was paid for them in the form of cattle. The more girls one had the more cattle he got upon their marriage and, therefore, the wealthier he became. Child mortality was very high due to lack of proper health facilities. This encouraged men to marry many wives to have many children, so that if any died in childhood some were left to grow to adulthood.

Many women married to the same man also provided a source of cheap labor so that the more women, the more production in the fields and, therefore, the richer the man. This was not necessarily so in some cases. If the women gave birth mostly to boys, this meant that the father was going to have less cattle. In order to deal with this misfortune, the sons had to go cattle raiding in order to acquire cattle to pay a dowry for their wives. Sometimes fathers gave their daughters in marriage to their friends as a sign of solidifying their friendship. If a woman got married and turned out to be barren, her younger sister was given to her husband in marriage with the hope that she would produce children for the family. The same was practiced if a married women produced children of one gender only.

Men with many wives were honored and treated with respect in their clan. Their opinion in the community was taken seriously. When land was to be divided, a bigger portion was allocated to a polygamous man than to a man with one wife.

In the olden days people who grew up in polygamous homes had strong psychosocial values. Children grew up in a life of sharing and fending for each other without discrimination. High standards of discipline were maintained, because any parent could discipline any child.

There are no statistics to prove this, but it was believed that the population of girls was greater than that of boys and so polygamy thrived. Many believed that in order to provide homes for all the girls, they had to marry more than one wife.

Many negatives resulted from polygamy. If a man failed to satisfy all his wives sexually, the women went astray and had children by outsiders. The man who was considered the head of the family was the only decision-maker and he never consulted with his wives in most cases. A reign of terror and dictatorship therefore prevailed in polygamous homes. Democracy was a foreign phenomenon. And so it is even in most African political structures today.

Competition for attention from the husband brought jealousy among the women. This gave way to acts such as witchcraft, betrayal, and constant verbal and physical fights among the women and children. This resulted in hatred and division among the members of the same family.

Many women died young as a result of trying to have too many children in a short time. Childbearing became a competition among women married to the same man. Many women also died young as a result of extreme physical labor, as they had to make sure their children were well fed and well taken care of.

When a man died his brothers and male cousins inherited all his wives. This promoted polygamy. Today, polygamy and wife inheritance pose a huge threat to the lives of the members of the Luo community, considering the fact that AIDS is mainly spread through sexual intercourse. The Luos are being forced by Mother Nature to review and change some of their cultural practices such as polygamy and wife inheritance. It must, however, be emphasized that from a social point of view, the Luos have a long way to go in developing adaptability to live religiously and harmoniously among themselves. Much more effort needs to be applied by all Luos in order to achieve increasingly higher levels of adaptability between the members of the Luo tribe.

More than ever before the Luos need to apply the fundamental biblical teachings of love for one another, going the extra mile, and all other fundamentals of social adaptability. Only in this way will Luos be able to develop the necessary social ability to survive. This is an essential requirement for the control of AIDS.

If there is to be a renewed drive for peace and prosperity within African families, then church leaders must be key actors in this drive. A renewed commitment to peaceful changes must be initiated right from the church.

And finally a quote from a Nigerian writer,

> Anyone who reflects on our traditional ways of speaking about morality is bound to be struck by the preoccupation with human welfare. What is morally good is what befits a human being; it is what is decent. What brings dignity, respect, contentment, prosperity, joy to man and his community. What is morally bad is what brings misery, misfortune and disgrace.

For Reflection and Discussion

1. Discuss the definition of peace by Thomas Aquinas. Does it cover what you think is important? What other good definitions have you heard?

2. Discover the characteristics of peacemaking by creating a list of ways to finish the sentence, "Peacemaking is...."

3. What underlying customs and beliefs tend to encourage the practice of polygamy in Africa?

4. Why is polygamy a concern for African peacemakers?

5. The author suggests that "peaceful changes must be initiated right from the church." If you were a church leader in Africa, how would you go about creating and making these changes?

6. Summarize what you have learned from this chapter.

Chapter Eight

Democratic Republic of the Congo and Zambia: *Umutende Mukwai*: Peace Please

By Bunda Chibwe

"Umutende mukwai" literally means "Peace please" or "Is there peace please?" This common and popular greeting means: Are you at peace in your mind? Are you healthy spiritually and physically, mentally and psychologically, politically and economically? Are you in peace in your family? Are the members of your nuclear family safe and sound? Are they enjoying good health? Are they related to each other in a dignified manner? Are you in peace in your neighborhood, in your nation, and your global village, this planet, the only place to enjoy life together?

"Umutende mukwai" therefore attracts attention to know how life is in the community. For us, to live is to be part of the community. When you disassociate from the community, your life will be ruined and in shambles. You become an island and lose your identity as a person. In Africa you are not valued for what you possess but for who you are as a person in the community.

The greeting also means: Do you have good news to share with us today? Are there things to be concerned about, things to combat in order to restore the peace we all long for? Is there a special need to be united for in order to establish a world full of life, harmony, blessed with love, joy, and justice?

Umutende mukwai, ("Is there peace please?") *Mwende umutende,* ("Go in peace") *Shalenipo mutende,* ("Stay in peace")—these greetings carry a wide range of meanings, which are similar to *shalom* in Hebrew/Jewish literature.

Like the Bemba (of the Democratic Republic of the Congo and Zambia), the Jews in the Old Testament understood peace as a state of wholeness—possessed by persons or groups—that may be health, prosperity, security, or the spiritual completeness of covenant.

The Jews did not make any separation between military and economic peace, between bodily and spiritual peace. Individual peace was synonymous with the good life of a person, the healthful sleep, length of life, prosperity, and a tranquil death after a full life. Communal peace was the group's prosperity and security, which implied that the economic and political prosperity of the people was bound together harmoniously to serve the people's interests. God was seen as provider and also as healer of wounds and sickness, which entered a society to destroy peace.

To the Jews, the religious peace was of God (Isaiah 45:7) and the condition of peace was the presence of God (Numbers 6:26, I Chronicles 23:25). It was therefore human righteousness under the covenant that made life peaceable. To be at peace was to be upright, an upholder of truth, and faith. It was to practice justice. The covenant of peace in the Jewish tradition involved a mutuality of relationship between God and the person, but at the same time conveyed Yahweh's blessing on humanity. This blessing would be applied to strengthen, to pardon sin, to bring joy, and to assure an answer to prayer.

Those who trusted God and hoped in God's salvation received peace from God. Although judgment and trouble could precede the actuality of eschatological peace, Israel knew that her suffering was the chastisement of peace, the stripes that brought about God's own healing.

In the New Testament the word "peace" was first used to describe the cessation or the absence of hostilities between rival groups. This understanding is found in Luke and an extension of this same meaning is found in Ephesians 2:14–17 where peace is the reconciliation Christ brought about between Jews and Gentiles, groups normally antagonistic to each other. It was equally used to mean peace of mind or serenity (See Romans 8:6, Galatians 5:22, and John 14:27) because the gift of peace is explicitly offered to appease, and stands in contrast to the troubled and fearful hearts of the disciples. In one sense the harmonious relationship is set forth as the goal of a Christian endeavor.

Similarly, in Bemba society, the word is also used to indicate harmonious relationship between God and people, husband and wife, and the people living in the same family.

What would you say if you were forced to pound your own baby, cook it and serve it, not only to your oppressors but also to yourself, as they continue to taunt you? What would you do if you were caught in the quarrel between a group of terrorist rebels and embattled home troops, both fighting to take your life? What would you do when soldiers are grabbing your civilian clothes and force you to wear their military uniform, surrender your guns, and leave you at the mercy of enemies? Imagine a situation where you scrounge for cassava skins and round worms for your survival. Nothing is more sorrowful than seeing your own child dying because you do not have fees to pay for the medical treatment of your child, although many good hospitals are available. How would you talk about peace, love, joy, and justice in this environment?

My brother-in-law, who escaped and survived the war in the Democratic Republic of the Congo, confirmed these instances. He first refused to eat food twice a day. He constantly jumped from his chair in fear, cried for help, and thought that people were still pursuing him to take his life. His eyes changed, becoming reddish, as he related the several incidences he went through during the war. Because he left his parents, brothers, and sisters behind, he calmly confessed to me, "If there is anything you could do to help me live a human life, please teach me how to make this world a peaceful place to live. I hate war. I will do and give everything I have to stop the bleeding." Finally he said, "I wish God were watching how people are dying and innocent people executed. Unfortunately, God is too far from us to listen even to the crying of the faithful and the righteous."

When people live in the culture of silence, when people are tamed and accept their fate as God's will, when people do not have anything else to do than to surrender to the mercy of chance and goodwill, their lives become meaningless and miserable. They lose hope, love, justice, and peace. They attack God rather than the human systems that alienate the dignity and essence of human existence.

Africa, like all the other continents on this planet, needs peaceful societies. By peaceful society, Bishop Dennis De Jong of Ndola Diocese means a community of people where harmony and positive relationships exist between all members of the society. Peace, he continued, is thus the mark not simply of individual well-being but of the way society itself is structured— its social, political, economic, and cultural institutions. This is why he associates peace with justice: the right order of society where the dignity and the rights of individuals are respected and the unity and development of people are promoted.

The bishop strongly believes that peace is not simply the absence of conflict but the presence of justice. To promote peace we must work for justice. The fact that there is an apparent civil calm and no visible disturbance in society by no means indicates it is a peaceful society. Rather, it may be an oppressed society where the cries of the unjustly treated are stifled and where people have given up hope for any change for the better.

Throughout history peace has had many different meanings and has been understood by people in various ways. In the nineteenth century the word peace meant a general belief in the desirability and possibility of a warless world. But by the turn of the twentieth century it was being used to denote active resistance to war, and by the mid-twentieth century it had narrowed down to signify a belief in nonviolence. Peace is regarded as a universal desideratum.

People as diverse as Ronald Reagan, Pietr Botha, my father in Mansa, and my mother in Lubunda talk peace. But it means altogether different things to different people. When there is no funeral in the village, or when the nurses are not on strike, there is peace. But what peace was U.S. President Reagan defending when he justified his invasion of the tiny island of Grenada in 1984? Which peace was Reagan after when he sent his warplanes to attack Libya in 1986? It is frightening to recall the number of people and governments who supported the invasion in the name of God and country.

Was the peace they sought for the strong and powerful, the rich, the high and mighty, to do as they please, unrestrained by law, custom, conscience, or international morality? Was it the peace of a superpower to do whatever it pleases and to pursue its own interests without regard to the interests, security, and concerns of other apparently weaker nations?

When Botha, the leading white supremacist and leader of apartheid in South Africa, said that he was for peace, people believed him. For him peace meant the acceptance of the status quo. Peace called for blacks and whites to be rigidly segregated in all aspects of their lives, with blacks occupying subordinate positions in all walks of life. Otherwise anything else would lead to conflict. Botha wanted peace only to continue to oppress the blacks of South Africa.

We are aware that several words are being used in the study of peace: agapeology, ahimsavarda, aresology, bellicosology, caritasology, heralogy, ireneology, pacology, and polemology. At the center of these nice vocabulary entries, the core problematic question should be addressed: peace for whom and peace for what?

The harsh conditions in Africa demand the search for a peace that will touch all possible dimensions of people's lives. Africa is longing for a lasting and meaningful peace. That peace should be multicausal and monocasual; both a means and an end; good for individual, family, and group; intra- and international; conditional and unconditional; immediate, limited, and permanent. It should be acceptable and practicable for both individuals and groups. We need a maximum, pragmatic, and evolutionary peace articulated and understood by Africans that fits their context. Rather than imported and artificial, we need an authentic, and indigenous peace.

While developed countries emphasize the threat of nuclear war and disarmament, as well as issues such as drugs and the environment, African countries would rather focus on issues such as the inherent injustice in the international economic system. Such injustices hurt the inhabitants of developing countries and do not get adequate exposure in peace literature.

Africa has suffered a great deal by the extent of the involvement of other governments. The United States and other Western governments have been unashamedly supporting authoritarian governments so long their leaders offer protection and security for foreign capital investments. If we regard democratic structures as desirable in themselves and as instrumental for achieving peace and stability, then we would expect Europe to support the initiatives (few and limited though they are at the moment) to create democratic structures that will make it possible for the mass of the people to have meaningful control over the political processes controlling and guiding their lives. This is the only way we can ensure peace and development in Africa.

It will not hurt to repeat myself here. Peace has been distorted by many factors. Once again, if peace is to be real and not simplistic, it should be conceptualized and perceived, not only in the negative sense of minimizing or resolving conflict but in the positive sense of creating material conditions that provide for the mass of the people certain minimum conditions of security, economic welfare, political efficacy, and psychic well-being.

Michelo Hansungule of Raoul Wallenberg Institute at the University of Lund in Sweden, in his analysis of the challenges of good governance in Zambia, enumerated the following as distractions for peace in Zambia. The factors may be true for other countries as well:

- ancient and ineffective legal system, undemocratic governance;
- defective electoral system and institutions, lack of transparency;
- lack of accountability in public service, poor human rights records;
- extremely deep level of poverty, insufficient quality donor support;
- some customary practices, continued prevalence of preventable diseases;
- the AIDS/HIV virus;
- absence of a social justice system;
- high level of unemployment, unsystematic retrenchment exercises; and
- poor economic system, the negative effects of the privatization program.

The Democratic Republic of the Congo, a country currently divided by civil war, recently retrenched 7,000 people from the copper mines without giving them any benefits whatsoever. What would prevent those people, who have been sent into the streets, from joining with the enemies of the government and fighting against such a government? Are those people going to eat the imported so-called democracy? When their children and relatives die, will the existence of an ineffective Senate and House of Representatives come to change the alarming conditions of life for them?

Yashpal Tandon noted that the major problems of Africa that threaten peace and regional security have their genesis in its relations with the outside world rather than internally generated ones (such as border conflicts). However, when it comes to cleaning the dirty clothes in the family, I would ally myself with the several distinguished participants of the 37th Dag Hammarskjold Memorial Seminar, who concluded that if peace is to be achieved in African countries with their current democratic experiences, the following will be needed:

From the NGOs (Nongovernmental Organizations)

1. Begin to carry out civil education on peace issues in communities and in schools.

2. Help to alleviate poverty, a bad egg to democracy.

3. Empower women and children so they can speak freely and advocate for their rights.

4. See to it that government creates employment for the youth, because they can turn into potential criminals if they are not employed.

5. Make sure that the government makes clear the implementation of the draft policy on women submitted in 1995.

From the Media

1. Write articles that are educative and informative on topics such as human rights, so that people can know about these issues and fight corruption.

2. Be a watchdog and write investigative stories exposing any misconduct in public affairs.

3. Report truthfully, fully, accurately, and factually.

4. Be accessible to all stakeholders so that all views can be heard.

5. Make sure the media performs its job professionally.

From the Churches

1. Be united and have a common platform on governance issues.

2. Be the conveyer for issues on governance and democracy because of the large representation of people.

3. Church ministers should become knowledgeable on human rights so they can teach their church members.

4. Give an ear to all political parties.

Education

1. Educational institutions should become culture centers where good morals can be taught.

2. Strengthen educational institutions that bring about good governance.

3. Widen moral teachings to include the community, home, school, and churches.

4. Introduce a syllabus that will equip children with trades before leaving primary and secondary schools.

5. Give leadership training to educators throughout their careers so that they can teach others.

Political Parties

1. Parliament: change rules and procedures in order to accommodate the true African way of expression and debate (e.g., not to use questions and answers but speeches). Make it easy for the public to attend debates and cheaper and easier to introduce private members' motions.

2. Power sharing: use the proportional power sharing as per percentage of seats won in parliament as provided for by the constitution. This builds and increases goodwill, togetherness, and, most importantly, coexistence, which is a must for both peace and good governance.

3. Institutions (such as judiciary, anticorruption, and media): have built-in authority to take initiative, conclude, and publish things on their own, without outside interference.

Human Rights and Democracy Organizations

1. Facilitate dialogue constantly.

2. Litigate or help litigate on behalf of those who are imprisoned for exposing corruption.

3. Lobby and advocate for greater powers for the Anti-Corruption Commission.

4. Promote private prosecution for the offenses of public officers.

5. Provide mass civil education for the electoral process to reduce apathy.

6. Present a workable and generally accepted alternative to the current electoral process.

7. Give lobbying skills to the people to enable them to ask for what belongs to them.

8. Strengthen the institutions of democracy and encourage political will in government to make these institutions work.

9. Encourage networking between both small and large civic educational institutions and NGOs to increase effectiveness and capacity building.

In view of the aforesaid, I would reiterate with Emmanuel Hansen that the perspective on the peace problem that Africans can defend and justify is what makes it possible for the majority of the people on this planet to enjoy physical security, a modicum of material prosperity, the satisfaction of the basic needs of human existence, emotional well-being, political efficacy, and psychic harmony. Hansen believes this will enable the masses of the world to develop their potential and, consequently, themselves as full and autonomous human beings. It will enable them to develop, not as means to other ends, but as ends in themselves.

I wish the OAU (Organization of African Unity) good luck as it continues to be faithful to its three main goals and objectives, among several others, in the area of crisis management. The first deals with the intrastate conflict, as is the case in about four countries now in Africa. We would like to see the OAU's commitment to the preservation of the status quo and the principles of the territorial integrity in those countries concerned with secessionist claims. The second is the interstate conflicts that are settled through the mediation of heads of states, who act as agents of dissuasion, inhibition, or pacification. President Chiluba is currently playing a vital role in solving the conflict in Democratic Republic of the Congo. The third is the prevention of foreign intervention in African disputes. Africa, through its excellent method of negotiation, common consent, and reaching consensus would play a vital and significant role to protect its countries from manipulation by foreign countries.

At the individual level, peace, if it has to be, is really up to us. We are all called to create peace, to work for it, to establish it, and to live it wherever we are. I encourage the continuing strengthening of our African strategy of referring a person troubled by various factors to someone of their own temperament for assistance to restore peace of mind. The community has always been at the forefront to ensure that each person is attended to and cared for no matter what.

At the family level, I would like us to continue the *"Ichikosha Lupwa"* Cottage to strengthen the family relationship. People with reconciliatory skills are called upon under the "village palace" to counsel and cement broken relationships in divided homes with the ultimate goal to restore peace in the family. The sharing of a meal together as a sign and symbol of reinforcing family ties and resolving conflict concludes the ceremony.

At the clan, tribal, and ethnic level, I still remember seeing the *chilolo* (counselors to the chief) negotiate and reach a compromise. At the end the clan in conflict shares the totemic food as a symbol of recognizing the differences between the clans but also to appreciate each other's way of perceiving things. The Luba in Mbuji Mayi shared dog meat with the Lulua of Kananga the time they had a severe conflict between them.

At the regional level, John Ostheimer suggests major surgery and resuscitative measures because the collective African machinery for meeting the challenges and threats to African sovereignty, stability, and solidarity has, over the years, proved to be generally ineffective. The main reason is that the program and action groups are still in their infancy, because the disturbance of peace in Africa and, at the same time, the roots of militarism go back to the period when Africa was opened up to the rest of the world. The African countries should develop a mechanism to resolve disputes among the members' states. Asante believed that the following should be equally addressed:

- The existing regional schemes should diversify their external economic relations.
- Preferential economic links need to be developed, first among themselves and, secondly, with integration schemes in the other developing countries.
- Introduce fundamental policy and institutional changes and strengthen the powers of the OUA secretary-general.

The secretary-general needs to be a good facilitator, an enabler, and a motivator who is constantly helping the various countries to raise their level of conscience awareness. He or she should commit to discuss issues of peace violation and militarist rule in the African countries that, for the most part, attained only political independence.

The Reorganzed Church of Jesus Christ of Latter Day Saints in Africa is on the forefront in the proclamation of Christ and in the promotion of communities of joy, hope, love, peace, and justice. The worldwide vision fostered through the Temple at its international headquarters is dedicated to the pursuit of peace, reconciliation, and healing of the spirit. Its ensign (drawn from Isaiah 65:25) testifies of the absolute value the church and its members are seriously engaged in to be a people doing the best they can to help God create a world blessed with peace.

Church members strongly believe they are commissioned to be peacemakers. Duane Couey is right when he states that peace lies at the heart of spirituality. It is an attitude of personal acceptance and harmony. Peace requires determination and commitment to action. The Young Peacemakers Club, implemented respectively in South Africa and Liberia by Mary Ooko and Oliver Seydenouh, is a convincing demonstration of the church to acknowledge that peace has to start with children if we want it to be effective, efficient, productive, and procreative. It demands that all of us work for it. Whatever my size, there are things I can do to make the world a better, more peaceful place.

For a church that values the worth of each person and whose missionary statement is to proclaim Jesus Christ, the call is for people to meet the needs of the person in all dimensions of life. Such a message creates shalom in the person. And a person at peace exhibits a truly serene, calm composure. Peace is humanity flourishing in all its dimensions.

It is mandatory for the church of Jesus Christ to advocate, live, and promote *"umutende, icibote, amani, shalom,"* because *umutende* means openness, mutual support, integrity, sensitivity to self, the family, the community, the nation, and the world. We may not agree with each other on an understanding of peace, but one thing is certain: we are all called and challenged to improve the political, economic, social, and cultural systems in the places where we live. By so doing we, in our different sense of calling, will create a world where people accept each other as human beings and feel responsible for the well-being and welfare of all. I am longing for and am proud to see that Saints are a people dedicated to create "Zion" with God where they are and where they live. Yes, we are a worldwide church dedicated to the pursuit of peace, reconciliation, and healing of the spirit.

For Reflection and Discussion

1. Create a list of elements of our lives that are important to us in order to have peace. Identify the five you think are most important to you. Identify the ones the author of this chapter and authors of other chapters would identify as most important.

2. Read the scriptures given from both the Old and the New Testament and explore their meanings. What other scriptures about peace are you familiar with? What differences and similarities do you find between the two testaments and today's understandings?

3. Is peace possible without justice? How do you define justice?

4. Consider how peace might be viewed differently if you were rich and powerful or if you were poor and powerless. Which group is most eager for change?

5. Look in an unabridged dictionary to learn the meaning of any unfamiliar words used in the study of peace. Add these to your discussion when appropriate.

6. In looking at the list of what needs to be done to achieve peace in Africa:
    a. Do any of the suggestions surprise you? Why?
    b. Are there any recurring themes?
    c. Would the same list work in another country?

7. After reading this chapter with its suggestions, imagine that you are an African and a member of the Reorganized Church of Jesus Christ of Latter Day Saints. Tell where or how you would begin working for peace.

Chapter Nine

India: Peace Is Lived

By Rupa Kumar

For centuries people have believed India to be a peace-loving country. Historically, scripturally, and culturally India has been claiming the enviable name of originator and an instrument of peace. But the fact that the concept of peace was considered so important itself indicates that there might have been a context of peacelessness, both in the past and in the present. The forces that work against peace probably have had an upper hand, resulting in the search for peace and the consequent experience of attempting to find a new path for peace.

I will make a sincere attempt to listen to the conflicting and contrasting voices from India that we believe will reflect the true status of peace, both as a concept and as an experience in India.

"Om shanthi" is a typical Indian phrase referring to eternal peace based on the understanding that everything shall come to an end and peace will prevail. Generally, peace was considered to be the absence of a conflict or a problematic situation. *Om shanthi* echoed throughout the subcontinent for centuries. All the saints and sages preached peace and retired to the forest, leaving actual participation in normal life. Being away from the busy world and meditating upon God, one expected to calm the mind and attain eternal peace. While this is the general pat-

tern of searching for peace, it still had several variations based on religion, language, and culture.

Contributions of Religions

While Hinduism is the major religion in India, other religious groups have also had a significant presence. From an outsider's point of view, India reflects Hinduism. But Hinduism itself is a collection of various sects and subsects based on pantheism. Everyone talks about peace. Creator, sustainer, and destroyer—every aspect of the Hindu concept of God is supposed to be doing its roles for ultimate peace and justice for all people. The vedic scriptures of the Aryans talked about peace for everyone, but they also divided people based on the caste system and left a portion of them as "out of caste," meaning they are not worthy to be treated as human beings.

The Dravidian culture, which had its own origin, has different views from Hinduism but is still immersed in the all-encompassing Hinduism. Establishing peace and justice through war and punishing the unjust were the central themes of both Ramayana and Mahabharatha, the great epic stories of India. Throughout history people have interpreted various concepts and ideologies from these epics to suit their own understanding of peace and justice based on their own values and beliefs. How much these interpretations help to unite humanity to develop equality and self-dignity based on peace and justice—instead of trying to divide people based on birth and rebirth, caste, and creed—still remains a question. "Take up the sword and fight the evil, punish them in order to bring peace and justice. In doing so you are fulfilling your duty as expected by God, do it without reflecting on the consequences which can be left to God" is the basic message of the Bhagavad Gita. We cannot oversimplify the theme and messages of these great epics and scriptures. But establishing a peaceful and just society appears to be the logical goal of the teachings found in the Bhagavad Gita. Hinduism has made major divisions like *saivaits* and *vaisnavites,* referring to the people who worship Shiva and Vishnu. Deeper religious studies will bring out the various aspects of these two sects.

From a very early time two distinct traits were discernable in the religious life of the people in India. One is ritualistic and other contemplative. The outcome of meditation and contemplation was expressed in the close conversations of the Upanishads. "Whatever there is, is the abode of the Supreme" declares the Isa Upanishads. It expresses the recognition of life embodied in every organism. Living, therefore, was a matter of peaceful relationship with the entire universe.

Oneness and harmony with everything in nature is projected again and again in Indian philosophy and artistic tradition. It is believed that there is no scope for the brutal force of violence when a person has attained the ability to feel the true harmony and a sense of oneness with everything surrounding him or her, whether animate or inanimate. It is this feeling of oneness with the universe that generates the concept of peace—peaceful coexistence based on nonviolence. We are encouraged to look at the universe, not in an egocentric context, but to perceive ourselves as a part of the great universe and to respect the harmony of coexistence, which is the foundation for the concept of peace from an Indian background.

This understanding radically changed the day-to-day life of the common person. As every action in life was expected to be in conformity with the concept of *Ahimsa*, vegetarianism came into existence as a logical consequence.

The introduction and spread of vegetarianism as a unique gift of India to the world is indeed a turning point in the history of humanity: when we learn to regulate our personal needs or taste to protect the right of existence for all other lives around us. This statement is found in Dhammapada, the Buddhist scripture: "As I am, so are these, as these are, so am I." This identifies us with other living creatures. "Let man not kill nor cause everyone to kill the other" became the foundation of the concept of peace for Indians.

Kings and Heros

In Karnataka State, southern India, in a village called Saravanabelagula, there is a statue, erected in the ninth century CE in memory of the life of King Bahubali, the son of Rishabanatha. The story goes that Bahubali's brother, Bharatha, received a bigger share of the kingdom from his father than he did. Bahubali challenged Bharatha and both decided to resolve their claim by a personal duel, rather than causing bloodshed in battle. Bahubali overpowered his brother Bharatha, lifted him in his arms, and was about to hurl him down to the valley. Suddenly his heart was filled with self-realization and sorrow for what he was about to do. He felt ashamed of the brutal expression of his violent nature and repented. He gave the whole kingdom to his brother, renounced the world, and for years performed penance so intensely that snakes crawled around and creepers grew around his body. The most crucial conversion of his mind is beautifully expressed as follows: "It is not the futility of the act, but the multiple injury of the intent—that is violence."

It is true that in all cultures all over the world, various religions and their subsects have waged war against each other in the name of defending their faith, which was supposed to be existing for the purpose of bringing peace and harmony among people. But, as a result of war, sometimes people have changed their minds. The intensity of suffering, loss of lives, destruction of property, and the pain of the post-war scenario in Kalinga transformed King Ashoka from being a glorious warrior to being an ambassador of peace, campaigning for the cause of *Ahimsa* (nonviolence). Like Apostle Charles Neff of the Restoration movement who took the gospel to far away lands, it was Emperor Ashoka who took the gospel of Buddha outside India and the Far Eastern countries.

The significance and influence of Emperor Ashoka was so great that the architects of modern India chose to remember him forever by affixing his *Dharma Chakra* (Wheel of Peace and Justice) right in the center of the Indian National Flag.

Hardly any king in the world has ever issued an order prohibiting the killing of animals. The sentiments of nonviolence in India are so deep rooted that as early as the third century BCE Emperor Ashoka of Pataliputra (modern Patna) announced the prohibition of killing animals on certain days. The Girna rock inscription says:

> The religion consists in good works in the non-omission of many acts of mercy and charity, unity and chastity [these are] to me the annointment of consecration. Towards the poor and afflicted, towards bipets and quadrupets, towards fowls of the earth and things that move in water, manifold have been the benevolent acts performed by me. Out of consideration for things inanimate even many other excellent things have been done by me. To this purpose is the present edict promulgated: let all pay attention to it (or take cognizance thereof) and let it endure for ages to come.

This could be the voice of peace and justice originating from India centuries before the birth of Christ.

The practice of such proclamations continued in the later period as well. Huen Tsang, the Chinese traveler, refers to a similar kind of proclamation by Harshavardha of Kanauj. He gave himself to religious duties. He prohibited the slaughter of any living creature. He set the example, and ordered all his people to abstain from eating meat and he founded *Sangharamas* wherever there were sacred places of religion.

Later, several kings influenced by Jainism issued what is known as *amari-patas,* proclamations of nonkilling. *Hemachandracharya* refers to the amari proclamation by Kumarapala. Later kings must have followed the practice as well.

Gujarat and Rajasthan areas were under great influence of the Jains. Jains appear to have occupied influential positions in the royal courts. Some ministers have almost become legendary figures because of their religious and artistic patronage. Magnificent Jain temples all over Gujarat and Rajasthan in the late medieval period testify to a rich patronage to Jainism.

The influence of the practice of nonkilling was so strong in society that even Akbar, the Muslim emperor, accepted it and declared that on certain days there should be no killing of animals in his kingdom, as reported in the *"Ain-I-Akbari."*

Jehangir issued an amari-pata to Muni Vijayasena Suri, who was invited to spend the monsoon in Agra. Jehangir continued the practice of amari started by his father.

Propagation of amari, or non-killing, was almost a passion with the Jain community. It is even possible that the Jains made payments to people who would be deprived of their livelihood because of amari. There is an agreement of a butcher with the Mahajan of Baroda that the butcher would not practice his profession on certain days of the month. Whatever that be, there is no doubt that a sizable part of the population of India keenly observed the principle of non-violence even from the earliest centuries.

Gandhi's Influence

Through the ages, mystics, saints, and reformers all over the world have preached nonviolence for individuals. The twentieth century took one stride further when nearly one-fifth of the population of the world opted to introduce nonviolence in the political field, under the leadership of Mahatma Gandhi. This war-weary world was looking for a path to peace. Gandhi revealed to them through his experiment that there is no path leading to peace, but peace itself is the path.

For the first time in history an ordinary man called Mohandas Karamchand Gandhi, an attorney at law, came to be known as Mahatma (the greatest soul) because of his struggle for social justice and for political freedom based on the ideals of nonviolence. He called this his experiment with truth that, when properly understood, can open up a totally new, highly dignified, peaceful path—not only for conflict resolution but also an experience of true human life.

Nonviolent non-cooperation was the call of this great individual. It became an institutional creed in December 1920 when nonviolence was declared the basic creed of the Congress Party at its Nagpur session when it was passed unanimously by the 14,000 people attending. "For the first time in history," the president of the Congress Sri. (Mr.) Vijayaragavachari observed, "instead of the President and leaders driving the people, the people drove him and the leaders."

The matter of supreme concern was nonviolence in the Freedom Movement. It was not only the freedom but the way it was to be attained. Every action had to be tested on the touchstone of nonviolence. The story of Satyagraha in India, therefore, was a story of advance and retreat and further advance. It was the story of a freedom movement, which was a great experiment in truth and nonviolence.

Gandhi reminded us that there exists within each person a power or energy equal to the force of an atom bomb—a loving power, a caring power, and a healing power for peace.

Later, influenced by Gandhi's leadership, Jawaharlal Nehru put forward *"Panchsheela"* for the peaceful coexistence of nations. It was accepted as a code of ethics for neighboring countries to live together to avoid conflict and war.

India's Constitution

Dr. B.R. Ambedkar's contribution in drafting the constitution of India is significant. This paved the way for India—despite the presence of contrasting elements of our culture and diverse affiliation to language and religious origins—to emerge as a successful democratic country. Under his leadership peace received a legal stamp in the constitutional framework of India.

It is relevant to note the preamble to the constitution of India:

We, the people of India, having solemnly resolved to constitute India into a Sovereign, Socialist, Secular, Democratic Republic and to secure to all its citizens: *justice,* social, economic, and political; *liberty* of thought, expression, belief, faith and worship; *equality* of status and of opportunity, and to promote among them all *fraternity,* assuring the dignity of the individual and the unity of the Nation; *in our constitutent assembly....do hereby adopt, enact and give to ourselves this constitution.* [emphasis added]

Today, after India has completed fifty years of its existence as a free country, the question uppermost in the mind is, How has India lived up to the ideal cherished by the Mahatma? Also, how has it fared as an independent country? The latter query becomes pertinent because the whole world has been watching the Indian experience of democracy with keen interest. This is the case for two reasons. First, the then newly independent nation opted for the democratic path to guide its affairs and destiny. And second, it faced a mighty task of rebuilding and reshaping a country of continental proportions that had just emerged from two centuries of exploitative colonial rule.

India's Achievements

India's performance in the past half century appears creditable in key areas. The second most populous country on the world map is today feeding its 980 million people without outside help thanks to the so-called "green revolution," which can be considered as an expression of the concept of peace. There can be no peace when people are hungry.

Science and technology have brought a good industrial base and a self-reliant economy with adequate defense set up to meet external threats. It is true that many Indians live in poverty. Also true however, is that there has been a rapid expansion of the middle class. Unlike most developing countries, India is still a functioning democracy and a reasonably humane society where the rulers are accountable to the legislature, the press is free and unfettered, and the judiciary is fiercely independent. The election commission, an autonomous institution, ensures free, fair, and impartial elections.

There have been regional tensions and other pulls and pressures. But the social and economic bonds of the Indians have proved to be too strong to be snapped. As pointed out already, people of different faiths have coexisted in India for centuries. *"Sarva Panth Samba"* (equal respect for all faiths) is part of India's social consciousness. Secularism still prevails as the anchor of India's unity. It could be said that differences of religion, ethnicity, caste, and languages of the order that India has, do not exist anywhere else in the world. On top of it all the traditional society and an economy frozen for hundreds of years are in the process of modernization. The result is a social and moral convulsion, perhaps unprecedented in the history of this land. In a complex world situation, India's contribution to the nonaligned movement and its stand on the Nuclear Nonproliferation Treaty and Comprehensive Test Ban Treaty are instances of India's invulnerability in foreign affairs. India is being acknowledged as an emerging power in its own right.

This emerging Asian tiger is unshackling its economy through liberalization and loosening the creative energies of its people. Very impressive! A great country with a great history, with a great constitution, India is expecting a great future.

India's Challenges

How does the average person "experience peace" in this great country of great traditions? What roles have the great religions, the great values, the political architecture, and the growth of the developing industrial economy played in the lives of the common man or woman on the streets of India? What can be seen in the way families live their day-to-day life?

The population explosion—two children born every three seconds—belittles all the achievements of modern technology. Ignorance, irresponsibility, selfishness, lack of vision, and absence of an overall national conscience add to the existing woes.

Dividing the country into different states for administrative purposes was an essential need of the late fifties. But when the divisions were made based on the languages spoken in different areas, it created a narrow vision and language affinity among the people, which could be the reason for the divisive forces and ethnic allegiances—sometimes at the cost of broad national interest.

In a country where more than twenty official languages and 200 dialects are spoken, the need for a national language becomes a big question. It causes further pain and anguish when a handful of states claim superiority and, in the name of the need for one national language, expect all the others to learn their language. It becomes an irritation when attempts are made to achieve it by force. The voice of peace and justice is feeble here.

Corruption in high places and its prevalence (practically to the last person) in government offices is becoming more or less an accepted phenomenon in India today.

Some political leaders amass wealth disproportionate to their known sources of income, while the common person is unemployed or underemployed. Qualified people go to foreign countries and accept jobs for much cheaper salaries than others because of compulsions at home. People with "black money" raise the cost of living in urban areas, which naturally affects the living conditions in a double-standard "pseudo-economy." The poor become poorer and the rich become richer. Honest people who are underemployed suffer in trying to make both ends meet. The temptation to get sucked into the local system of corruption is so strong that the internal peace of mind for the individual and family are at stake. Where shall we start preaching about peace and justice?

It is like fighting an internal war of values, which surely has its external implications. How we behave in society and what guides us to make decisions in life are the external result of how we are anchored internally. Our spiritual convictions, the source of our internal strength, our capacity to understand, and the interpretations of our experiences with the Supreme One will be expressed in our lifestyle. Now what is the source for common people in India to have this experience of peace and justice?

Caste System

The religions of India have failed us. They teach, preach, and practice the sort of values we see in action in society today. Christianity is supposed to have offered some values in a caste-ridden society. But what can be done when one set of Christians strongly believes that Jesus belongs to *their* particular caste? There have been cases in our own church where a priesthood member's appointment is not accepted by the local congregation simply because the pastor was from an untouchable community. Construction of churches has been stopped halfway through because those who did not accept the theory that Jesus belongs to the Nadar community have been expelled by the majority group. There have been separate seats allotted to the members who were converted to Christianity from "lower caste" groups of Hinduism.

History is full of irrationalities. How many churches have conducted their worship service with police protection and their Communion service with the highest security? The message of Christ is of love, self-sacrifice, and selfless service to humanity. So we find the picture or image of the historical Jesus kept respectfully along with the pantheon of gods in any Pooja Room (Prayer Room) of most Hindu households. But what about Christians? Christians are generally believed to be identified with the low caste and hence, in several areas, they are not able to get houses to rent. This is not explicit but an unwritten tradition in society, which makes life miserable and Christians angry. In that sense some would say the Hindus are not worthy of love, affection, or friendship. What, then, will happen to the call for peace and justice?

The Dalits (untouchables) have their own painful struggle. Women are treated as objects given as a gift to the bridegroom so she may lose her virginity in marriage, which alone will entitle her to enter into heaven and rest in peace after death. Hence the man is next to God! The parents of girl children must do everything and give everything to please the bridegroom so he will be pleased to help the bride attain *Moksha* (heaven). Thus came the dowry system. In certain cases, those who do not bring enough dowry are burned alive. Women are tortured to bring more and more every time there is a need for the man. When unable to provide a dowry for more girl children, female infanticide is practiced. The voice of the female fetus cries louder than the voice of Christianity in India.

Serving others as a way of life has been the model shown by the Christian missionaries to India. They gave the Indians education, health care, and awareness of equality. They refined the national conscience on social justice. But words cannot express the grief experienced when an Australian Christian missionary, the Reverend Mr. Steins, and his two children were burned alive for no valid reason except for religious fanaticism—even though for decades they had served a leper community. Christ spoke aloud when Mrs. Steins was willing to forgive the killers and appealed to the authorities not to hurt them.

The Challenge of Peacemaking

Is there a time or season, a logic or situation where peace can be initiated? Peace is within. Let our cups overflow. In the situation we saw in India there could be every reason for one to think that practicing the Christian life is very difficult. The feeling that "so much needs to be done and I cannot do anything" is not Christian.

Taking the first step, like Moses did in faith, is the need of the hour. The global condition can be shaped by our individual, local action. The very small step to take action on a particular small need can be transformed into a mighty force answering the call of people to God to help them. And if we are able to initiate any process that will become an instrument of peace, God will surely bless and be with us in our attempt to be used in his hands. The magnitude of the problem need not discourage us. If we are willing to start doing something to make a difference in bringing peace and justice in our given context, that would do. God does not expect us to do everything all by ourselves. God is with us, and we need not be overly concerned about the methods we use. God will justify us, as long as our actions are in line with scriptural instructions, church experience, prophetic direction by leaders, and an inner guidance of the Holy Spirit—even as we pray about what we plan to do. It is not what we have done that is important, but what we have to do and where we have to go from here.

Peace is not given; peace is lived. It permeates itself even as we try to become peacemakers ourselves. It is possible only when we are anchored strongly in the faith and experience the holding of our hand by Jesus, even when we feel we are about to sink. It cannot be explained but must be experienced!

For Reflection and Discussion

1. Make a list of Indian words used by the author. Try pronouncing the words aloud and note definitions or English translations, if given.

2. What do you know about the caste system in India? How do you think it developed? How should peacemakers respond to culturally engrained systems like the dowry and caste systems?

3. Discuss how vegetarianism and not killing animals relates to the issues of peace.

4. The author mentions two common approaches to peace—ritualistic and contemplative. Discuss how these might be expressed in other settings and times. What additional approaches have authors of this book mentioned? Which approach is most desirable to you?

5. Why was King Bahubali made a hero in southern India? What legends and heroes of peace are there in your own culture?

6. Discuss the role and effectiveness of nonviolence as a proactive stance of peacemaking in India and other countries of the world. Where have you seen proactive nonviolence working?

7. The author created a list of India's accomplishments in becoming a nation of peace and a list of problems still needing work. Create such lists of achievements and challenges for your own country.

8. What insights on peace have you gained from reading this chapter?

Chapter Ten

Japan: Reflection on Peace

By Hiroshi Yamada

The mountains where we chased hares,
the streams where we fished the baby roaches,
come back and back in the dreams even today,
in our hearts remains the home we spent our childhood days.

How is my father, and how is my mother?
Hope they are doing well, the mates I played together.
When the rain falls or the wind blows,
it reminisces me of the home I spent my innocent days.

When I accomplish my dreams someday,
I shall return to my home far away,
to the home with blue mountains,
and with clear streams.[1]

This is one of the songs that are loved by many Japanese. In the early morning of a day during summer vacation, I was still in bed and heard my mother cutting some vegetables on the chopping board. She was making miso soup for breakfast. I smelled the sweet fragrance of the miso soup from the kitchen. I heard a bugle of the tofu vendor outside and I realized the day had already begun. Yet I was dozing in assurance that Mother was within my reach, which made me feel safe and at peace as if I were tucked in her bed. Years flew by. Father is gone now; so is Mother. But in my memories the mountains are still as blue as the ocean and the streams still run as clear as a mirror. Home far away brings back the fond memories of the days I was so innocent and of the peace I so much enjoyed. No matter how many years elapse, we still remember vividly the peaceful and innocent childhood days we spent with the family and friends far away at home. Home is the place where our hearts and minds fostered love, peace, and hope, and it is the place where our souls finally rest, joining with those of parents and ancestors after a long earthly journey.

There is no one in the world who likes war. Everyone, I believe, loves peace and seeks for peace. The Japanese are no exceptions. The art of flower arrangement, meditation gardens, and tea ceremony depict their spirit yearning for inner peace, as well as environmental peace. However, this spirit is often betrayed for one reason or another by the powers that are far beyond those of individuals, and we find ourselves in the midst of miseries. Such is the case for the Japanese in the 1940s.

Roots of War

Japan is the only nation in the world to experience the cruelties of the atomic bomb. It was estimated that 100,000 people, 30 percent of the total population of Hiroshima-city, were killed instantly by the blast. Another 100,000 were injured and, by the end of the year, another 14,000 more died from radioactive contamination. Even those who survived the nightmare of the blast and fires continued to suffer from various diseases such as anemia and leukemia. Mothers lost their babies in flames. Wives found their husbands dead under the debris. Many children became orphans without a place to live or go back to. Most cities in Japan had been destroyed by the end of the war—burned to ashes and mounds of debris—and the figures of the dead had totaled up to 672,000. Mountains turned brown, and the streams turned red. People lost their homes. What led Japan to such devastation?

Advancement of science and technology in the fifteenth century enabled Spain and Portugal to expand their colonies to India and the American continents for trading purposes. Spain invaded the Philippines (1571), conquered both Aztec (1521) and Inca Empires (1533)—forcing the natives to work as slaves in the gold and silver mines and on the farms. Portugal, on the other hand, arrived in India, where they occupied Ceylon [Sri Lanka], Maracas, Kang Tung, Maccau in China, and finally reached Japan in 1577. Very soon, with the Portuguese merchants, many Catholic missionaries came to Japan to proselytize people. Some feudal lords were converted to Christianity, and the people in their domains followed the lords. It became a tremendous threat to Japan, which was in the process of unification for the first time in its history. Thus Christianity was banned in 1600, and the missionaries were expelled. Japan closed the door to the world for the next two and a half centuries.

During that time the political and economic hegemony over the world market shifted from Spain and Portugal to Britain, France, and Germany. A newly emerging nation, the United States of America, was pushing its way to the international market. They were in competition with each other to expand their own colonies in Africa, India, Southeast Asia, and Far East Asia. Colonization was not always carried out in peaceful ways, but rather in brutal ways. In China, for instance, Britain smuggled opium from India to China for their benefit. When China laid an embargo on opium and their people protested against Britain, British armed forces opened fire against them—thus the Opium War broke out. For Great Britain to defeat China was as easy as twisting a baby's arm, because Great Britain was one of the leading powers of the West at the time and China was far behind in everything compared to the rest of the world. As a result China was forced to sign an unequal treaty with Britain in 1843.

Under such an international climate Japan was forced to open the country by the military threats of Commodore Perry, which followed the same types of unequal treaties in 1854 and 1858. It was an unforgettable humiliation Japan could never forget, and it aroused first a sense of urgency to strengthen military powers to cope with the threats of the West and, second, a sense of urgency to internally unify the nation before there were any external threats.

Japan spent nearly half a century catching up with the science and technology of the West. It was not to be devoured by colonialism. Yet it is ironic that by the turn of the century, Japan became strong enough to join the West in colonial exploitations. In fact, Japan expelled all the Western powers from Asia, Southeast Asia, and the Pacific, and declared itself to be the suzerain nation of the Greater East Asia Co-Prosperity Sphere. Japanese leaders taught their people to be proud of their race as being superior to any other races of the world.

Having been confined to small islands for more than two centuries without exposure to the world, the people believed what their leaders told them. They believed that the only way by which peace would be maintained was for inferior races to be subjected to the superior race. However, in reality such a concept of *Japanese supremacy* and peace was just a demagogue authored by a handful of people with endless desires for international markets. There were a few people who knew the real intents behind the government policies and propaganda. But the bureaucrats who ganged up with greedy capitalists took full control of politics, education, military, and police. As a result, the people were deprived of the freedom of press, speech, and assembly. Those who dared to raise questions were liquidated. The voice of protest was suppressed, and the hands of inquirers and objectors were ripped off. Everything was decided by someone in some place far distant (where, they knew not) and no one had a right to know the truth.

When the Japanese say "No more Hiroshima," many Americans often react immediately with "We do not forget Pearl Harbor." However, "No more Hiroshima" is not necessarily anti-American propaganda. It is rather an appeal to the world for an awareness of more basic problems that could lead them to such devastation as Hiroshima, Nagasaki, and Pearl Harbor at any time and any place. In other words, it implies that the tragedies of Hiroshima and Pearl Harbor happened neither just in a vacuum nor like a bolt out of the blue. There was a long history of keen competition between Japan and the Western powers as to who would control the markets, particularly of Asia and the Pacific, which were mostly undeveloped and un-protected. This competition was behind the scenes and many people did not realize what was happening. There was endless greed of a handful of leaders over untapped natural resources in those areas. A long history of ignorance and indifference about other peoples and their cultures did nothing but help develop false perceptions of the counterparts as *barbarians*. Colonial-ism intentionally instigated such racial prejudice and planted a superiority complex, taking advantage of people's ignorance, and justified depriving the dignity and the right of other na-tions and their people.

It is undeniable, and natural as well, that there are those who become emotional when they react to each other with these words about Hiroshima—particularly those who lost their loved ones in war actions, in bombings, or otherwise. There would probably be no other way to express their deep feelings. Yet, exchange of emotions in such a way would not promote peace. Healing needs to be taking place on each side so that Japanese can freely say "No more Hiroshima" and Americans can ami-cably say "We do not forget Pearl Harbor"—not as an attack to their counterpart but as a logo for mutual commitment to "No more wars, but peace." Time has come for us to move history ahead for the future.

Wars are currently being waged in many places in the world even at this moment; some are in the name of political inde-pendence, some in the name of religious integrity, and others in the name of ethnic cleansing. Incredible hatred among those concerned has been created and instigated. We often see on tele-vision the youth, men, and women—even small children—shouting against their enemies with their fists raised high as if

121

they were obsessed by something. But who will benefit by such hatred, wars, and territorial expansion—those young people, men and women, or children who appear on television? But aren't they the very ones who would lose their living quarters by bombings, food rationing, or their own or loved ones' lives by actions of hate?

The Peace Movement

Peace has always been a very important issue for Japan since the mid-nineteenth century, as previously mentioned. Various groups were actively involved in the peace movement: Buddhists, Christians, politicians, scholars, students, labor unions. However, all of those who were interested in peace did not necessarily share the same outlook on the ways to bring forth peace. During the cold war following the end of World War II, the Japanese peace movement was divided into two; one sided with the so-called communist-bloc nations, and the other sided with the so-called democratic-bloc nations. The former believed Marxism to be the basis for peace and the latter believed it was democracy. The peace movement was always coupled with political and economic issues closely related with more jobs, more rice, and more money. They argued vehemently with each other. However, the more affluent the society became, the less urgent the issues became.

When the Persian Gulf War broke out in 1991, Japan did not send its military troops because the Japanese Constitution prohibits armament.[2] Some people thought that peace should come by talks no matter what, and others thought that peace sometimes would not be obtained without military forces. Because of the constitution and prevailing public opinion, Japan supported the war indirectly through funding. There were many nations, including the United States of America, that did not think the monetary contribution was sufficient and that Japan should send troops.

Recently the People's Republic of Korea (North Korea) launched missiles toward Japan. North Korea's fishing boats, without fishing equipment and national flags[3] were often in the territorial waters of Japan. Such an international climate surrounding Japan makes public opinion gradually change. Although some are still against any kind of military action, more and more people feel it necessary to rearm the country for national defense.

As long as war is waged far from our own nation, it might be easy to talk about no military actions or peaceful negotiations. But for the countries whose sovereignty is threatened, whose motherland is being trampled down, whose kindred are killed or massacred in front of their eyes, peace issues become an urgent matter—whether to fight for integrity and freedom, or to die with shame and chagrin. Thus they may feel compelled to stand up with arms against the invaders to defend their nation, their lives, and their families—even though they would agree to sit before the table for peace talks. It is not a theoretical subject of faraway countries where they have never been.

The pursuit of peace is multifaceted and cannot be dealt with as simply a black or white issue. It is more complicated than we think, and therefore it cannot be accomplished simply by emotional appeals. It requires a revolutionary transformation of politics and economy. But at the same time it requires religions of strong determination to encourage active involvement and transformation in bringing forth peace to humans in terms of their own lives and the world in which they exist. Because this is not a paper for political science, I will focus on the latter subject rather than on the former one.

A Folktale

Junji Kinoshita, although he was not a Christian, was acutely aware of inherent human sin, which impedes the realization of peace when he rewrote *"Tsuru no Ongaeshi"*[4] for a play. Once there lived a poor farmer, Yohei. While at his small patch of farmland one day, he saw a crane, which was dying from injuries. He felt sorry, carried it home, and treated it with herbs. The wounds were cured several days later, and the crane flew away home. In a few days a beautiful woman appeared at Yohei's doorsteps. To make the story short, they married.

One evening the wife said to Yohei, "I am going to weave at the loom in the next room tonight, but promise me not to peek into the room so that I will not be distracted while I am working." Yohei understood and promised that he would never peek. Next morning the wife came out of the room with a piece of beautiful cloth and told Yohei to sell it in the town. He did as he was told and made much money.

He became very happy and asked her to weave more. The more she wove, the richer he became. As a result the poor farmer no longer needed to toil and moil on his little farmland. The wife began looking tired, but she continued to weave, because her husband wanted more cloth—the material she wove was so beautiful that many people wanted to buy it. One night Yohei could not inhibit his desire to find out how his wife made such a wonderful material. He broke his promise with his wife and peeked into the next room. What Yohei saw there, however, was not his wife but the crane whose life he had saved months ago. The crane was making the cloth with her feathers, most of which were now already gone. Every time the crane plucked a feather, blood came oozing out of her slender body. Yet she was weaving a cloth with her last strength.

Yohei saw what he should not see. The wife returned to being a crane and flew away with its frail figure. Yohei, with such a loving and caring heart that he could not just walk away when he saw an injured crane, loved his beautiful wife very much. But when he realized that she had unusual skill to produce beautiful cloth, by which he could make money, the tragedy began.

A relationship between husband and wife that should be as pure as *"I and Thou"* degenerated into *"I and It"*.[5] His wife was turned into just a tool for the pursuit of his own greed. Greed makes humans blind, insensitive, indifferent, and even cruel. Yohei did not see his wife becoming weak and weary. He could not see or did not want to see the (bleeding) sacrifices his wife was making behind the scene. Kinoshita depicted the sin inherent in the depth of human beings through a genre of literature.

Sin

There is no such concept of "God as lawgiver" in Japanese culture. Therefore, naturally there is no concept of covenant relationship between human and God. Where there is not such a covenant relationship, it is apparent there is no room for the Japanese to perceive sin as a breach of the covenant with God. This is a fundamental difference that makes what the Western culture is on one hand and what the Japanese culture is on the other.

It does not mean, however, that the Japanese do not have a concept of sin. They do have a concept of sin. For instance, they have a concept of *"three evils,"* which is often called "three poisons": greed, anger, and ignorance. To seek for things more than what we need is greed. To lose our temper over things that we do not like is anger. Ignorance is a perversion that leads us to think we are an absolute being, although we are a transient and relative being. By absolutizing ourselves, we intend to control the world and those around us at our own will. The world may come to an end, yet we intend to rule the world. We may die tonight and be buried tomorrow in a three-foot by seven-foot lot in a cemetery without anything to take with us. Yet we intend to gain fame and seize the power and wealth of the world. To accomplish these dreams we cannot be compassionate but have to be firm, competitive, manipulative, indifferent, insensitive, and intolerant. However, when we treat the world in this way, the world will turn against us with enormous power—uncertainties, anxieties, failure, fear, revenge, illness, death. We build up anger, not only toward ourselves but also toward the world that is not as controllable as we think.

"Tsuru no ongaeshi" ends with a scene of the wife, who is now turned back into a crane, fading away into the sky with its frail figure. Kinoshita seems to tell us ardently through this story that Yohei lost the most important thing in life, that is, the pure

relationship as husband and wife, and the deep love of his wife who did not matter yet who sacrificed herself for him. But his greed had blinded him. To be more fatally tragic, Yohei was so blinded he did not realize what he was until he broke the promise with his wife. When he came to himself, it was too late! He had already lost his wife along with love, trust, and devotion.

We tend to absolutize those things of transient nature, which are not absolute, including "self." Likewise, we tend to absolutize what we are and what we want, and place them in the center of the world and try to control the world and those around us under that "prerogative." Such ignorance and perversion is the sin deeply inherent in humans. How many tragedies have we experienced in and out of our lives because of this ignorance and perversion—massacre and genocide by ethnic exclusivism, divorces and violence over petty disagreement, sexual abuses and exploitation for selfish carnal desires, and trespasses on personal and corporate or international levels? Our societies are filled with those tragedies. Our history, yesterdays, and even this moment, are filled with such tragedies stemming from ignorance and perversion.

We look up in the sky in the direction where the crane flew away today and ponder on how painful it was for the crane to leave Yohei behind, for the pure-hearted crane wanted to return thanks to Yohei who had saved its life.

Therefore I tell you, do not worry about your life, what you will eat or drink; or about your body, what you will wear. Is not life more important than food, and the body more important than clothes? Look at the birds of the air; they do not sow or reap or store away in barns, and yet your heavenly Father feeds them. Are you not much more valuable than they? Who of you by worrying can add a single hour to [your] life?

And why do you worry about clothes? See how the lilies of the field grow. They do not labor or spin. Yet I tell you that not even Solomon in all his splendor was dressed like one of these. If that is how God clothes the grass of the field, which is here today and tomorrow is thrown into the fire, will he not much more clothe you, O you of little faith? So do not worry, saying, "What shall we eat?" or "What shall we drink?" or "What shall we wear?" For the pagans run after all these things, and your heavenly Father knows that you need them. But seek first [the kingdom of God] and his righteousness, and all these things will be given to you as well. Therefore do not worry about tomorrow, for tomorrow will worry about itself. Each day has enough trouble of its own.—Matthew 6:25–34 NIV

In Jesus, God and humans, humans and nature, person and person, person and "self" are not hostile to each other but are in peaceful and harmonious relationship. In the gospel of Jesus Christ we see that humans and the world are together in the bosom of God, just like we feel when we are in the bosom of nature at home far away. Trees in the mountains, streams in the vales, birds of the air, the lilies of the field bring us back to who we really are and who we really ought to be.

That is probably why this particular passage in the Bible is so familiar to Japanese. We love it, even though many are not Christians. Somehow it relates us to our old favorite song, "The mountains where we chased hares...." As the words pour out of our hearts, our eyes fly in an arc with the distant birds, butterflies, and locusts; and our minds travel back to the blue mountains, clear streams in the vales, and the fields at home. Our past, which is filled with greed, anger, and complacence, is washed away by the tears in reminiscence, and our souls are refreshed with peace, love, and hope for tomorrow.

For Reflection and Discussion

1. What brought the feeling of peace to you as a child? How has that changed?

2. What arguments were used to support dropping the atomic bomb? If you had been Japanese, how would those arguments have sounded to you?

3. What have been the results of one race, ethnic group, or religion feeling superior to another? Give interpersonal, community, and international examples.

4. List basic causes for conflict that the author has named. Add

reasons given by other authors. What ways can you suggest to change these basic causes in a way that will create peace?

5. Summarize your understanding of the Japanese view of sin. How is this alike or different from your own understanding of sin? How is it alike or different from the other countries you have been reading about? What does sin have to do with peace or the lack of peace?

6. What key ideas will you remember and use from this chapter?

Notes

1. Translated by the author.
2. General Douglas MacArthur created the Japanese constitution and presented it to Japan in 1945. It has been called "Peace Constitution" because its seventh chapter stipulates Japan's total renunciation of armaments.
3. International law requires any boats on the open sea to hoist their national flag for identification.
4. "Requital of a Crane," a Japanese folktale.
5. See *I and Thou* by Martin Buber (1978).

Chapter Eleven

The Prophetic Task of Engaging with Culture

By Andrew Bolton

Introduction

I have been fascinated reading these essays on different cultural perspectives on peace. This is without a doubt the most international book written in the history of the Restoration movement and a very significant one. The international church is genuinely coming of age and this volume is an exciting contribution as we see seek to become a movement dedicated to the pursuit of peace, reconciliation, and healing of the spirit.

It has been edifying to see how many of the authors have engaged with their culture in critical ways. I was touched by how Mary Ooko tackled polygamy head on in her own culture and with a woman's sense of outrage at this form of exploitation. Hiroshi Yamada with a poet's sensitivity speaks judgement of his own culture and nation and forces us in the West to confront our own participation in imperialism and racism. Rick Sarre, with clarity honed by professional scholarship, deals candidly with the violations of guns and native peoples and explores alternative forms of criminal justice. Kerstin Jeske Kristiansen and Eva Erickson tell the moving story of how churches effectively engaged in nonviolent resistance in their East German culture, culminating in the tearing down of the Berlin Wall. Etienne Faana helps us see into the communal ways of Tahitian society, which leads me to question the individualism of my own. Bunde Chibwe is hard hitting in his criticism of the devastation caused in Africa by colonialism and neocolonialism. At the same time he speaks of his hope in the gospel. Rupa Kumar, a courageous worker for women's human rights in Madras, India, is appreciative and critical of Hinduism and Christianity. Barbara Higdon focuses more narrowly but in significant depth on alternative ways of resolving conflicts in her native U.S. culture. Joseph Charlie brings insight and honesty about the interaction of culture and the gospel in his native Nigeria.

As an Englishman I love my language and literature, soccer and cricket, my country's landscape and flowers, and its Christian traditions of ethical nonconformity found in the Congregationalists, Baptists, Quakers, and Methodists. I rejoice in my country's developing pluralism. As a family we really enjoyed living in inner-city Leicester, a city where half the children are from ethnic minorities. I am proud of our unarmed policemen and the National Health Service with virtually free medical treatment for all according to need, including free emergency treatment for visitors from overseas. Anglican Archbishop Temple is reputed to have said in the 1940s that our commitment to a health system for all was the most Christian thing we had ever done.

Yet I also feel personally ashamed at the violence and injustice my small nation has inflicted on the world in its creation of an empire that exploited a quarter of the globe in its heyday. The industrial revolution, which began in my nation, was funded by profits from the slave trade. These slaves, amidst the tears and unimaginable suffering of humans torn from family and home in Africa, picked the cotton in America that supplied the textile mills of Lancashire. It is in Lancashire that I was born and grew up—both sides of my family benefited from the Lancashire cotton industry.

All of this is by way of introduction to the main purpose of this concluding essay: to explore the prophetic task of engaging with culture. I define culture as the way of life for a people.

It includes language, stories, beliefs, values, institutions, and technology. In exploring the prophetic task of engaging with culture I want to consider two questions:
- What does it mean to be a prophetic people?
- What is a possible agenda for prophets today?

What Does It Mean to Be a Prophetic People?

The Hebrew prophets reveal what it means to be a prophet. A prophet is one sent to speak justice, God's justice, to a people and their culture. Consider first the call of Moses:

> Then the Lord said, "I have observed the misery of my people who are in Egypt; I have heard their cry on account of their taskmasters. Indeed, I know their sufferings, and I have come down to deliver them from the Egyptians, and to bring them up out of that land to a good and broad land, a land flowing with milk and honey....So come, I will send you to Pharoah to bring my people, the Israelites, out of Egypt."
>
> —Exodus 3: 7–8, 10 NRSV

Hear Isaiah:

> Wash yourselves; make yourselves clean; remove the evil of your doings from before my eyes; cease to do evil, learn to do good; seek justice, rescue the oppressed, defend the orphan, plead for the widow.
>
> —Isaiah 1:16–17 NRSV

And see how Amos judged a religious culture:

> Hear this word, you cows of Bashan who are on Mount Samaria, who oppress the poor, who crush the needy, who say to their husbands, "Bring something to drink!"....
>
> I hate, I despise your festivals, and I take no delight in your solemn assemblies. Even though you offer me your burnt offerings and grain offerings, I will not accept them;.... Take away from me the noise of your songs; I will not listen to the melody of your harps. But let justice roll down like waters, and righteousness like an everflowing stream.
>
> —Amos 4:1, 5:21–24 NRSV

I see this prophetic tradition being lived out in the life of Jesus as he confronted his own culture and spoke against participation in systems and actions that violated the sacred worth of persons. When challenged by the religiously devout as his hungry disciples plucked ears of wheat on the sabbath, Jesus said:

> "Have you never read what David did when he and his companions were hungry and in need of food? He entered the house of God, when Abiathar was high priest, and ate the bread of the Presence, which it is not lawful for any but the priests to eat, and he gave some to his companions." Then he said to them, "The sabbath was made for humankind, and not humankind for the sabbath."—Mark 2: 25–27 NRSV

The sabbath institution was originally created for a people who had escaped from slavery. It was to be a day of rest equally for all (Deuteronomy 5:12–15). It was a cultural institution for blessing humans. When understandings about the sabbath did not serve human good, Jesus challenged them: "The sabbath was made for humankind, and not humankind for the sabbath." Likewise Jesus challenged the whole temple system. Intended to be a house of prayer for all nations, it had become a den of thieves in which the priestly aristocracy, under the cloak of religion, ripped off the poor in collaboration with the Roman taxation system. Religious and imperial taxes could take 40 or 50 percent of a poor peasant's income.[1] As Jesus angrily cleansed the temple in a prophetic action (Mark 11:15–19 and parallel passages) we glimpse the anger and sorrow of God at human perversion.

"The sabbath was made for humankind, and not humankind for the sabbath." Culture is made for humans, not humans for culture. When our cultures (stories, language, values, institutions, and technology) serve and express the equal worth of persons, then God's will is being revealed. When a culture violates any human, especially the vulnerable, then we are confronted with the judgment of God.

The story of the people of Israel is a prophetic story. Prophetic leadership freed the enslaved Hebrews from the exploitation of Pharoah. At Mount Sinai prophetic leadership presented God's teaching, the Torah, a new constitution for a freed slave people, to help the poor, to reduce slavery, to protect the vulnerable, to respect the stranger. The people of Israel were not to repeat with one another what they had suffered at the hand of Pharoah. Some have called the giving of the Law at Mount Sinai a "second exodus," this time not from slavery to the promised land, but from an old culture of exploitation and death to a new culture that saves and enhances all of life. The amazing thing about the people of Israel is not that they frequently faltered but that they institutionalized the role of prophet and allowed themselves to be called back to the original vision of *shalom*—God's peace and righteousness.

The spirit of prophecy is the song of the worth of persons. This is the spirit that challenges what is cruel, oppressive, or dehumanizing. We see this spirit of prophecy in the Hebrew prophets. It is in this tradition that Jesus unmistakably stands. Luke portrays this vividly when Jesus, at the beginning of his public ministry, is given the scroll of Isaiah, one of the greatest of the prophets. Jesus read this:

> The Spirit of the Lord is upon me, because he has anointed me to bring good news to the poor. He has sent me to proclaim release to the captives and recovery of sight to the blind, to let the oppressed go free, to proclaim the year of the Lord's favor. —Luke 4:18–19 NRSV (compare Isaiah 61:1–2 and 58:6)

This is the scriptural manifesto of Jesus, his vision statement, his mission purpose. We cannot understand Jesus if we do not understand his passionate commitment to creating out of his culture what will save the poor, free the captive, ennoble the despised, include the outcast, heal the sick, and serve all humans equally.

As we seek to become a worldwide movement dedicated to the pursuit of peace, reconciliation, and healing of the Spirit, then this prophetic task is for all of us in every family and congregation in every land. In the story of the Hebrew prophets and the life of Jesus, we have a model of engaging creatively and redemptively with culture. We are called to be more than a people with a prophet. We are called to be a prophetic people. God called the prophets of Israel so that all of Israel might be a light and blessing to the Gentiles. Jesus calls us to be a prophetic people so that we might be salt, a city of light on a hill (see Matthew 5:13–16).

How can we be a prophetic people? I discern the following method from the biblical tradition:

- Listen to the voices and tears of those who are hurting and let that pain touch us. See the statistics of war and poverty and imaginatively see the persons they represent.
- Hear God's call to liberate the suffering and oppressed from their pain and the causes of their hurt.
- Confront the powers, institutions, and values that oppress and exploit, be it government, bureaucracy, business, the military, multinational corporations, or the local school.
- When repentance begins, when the truth is being heard, when the victims find healing and new hope, then seek mercy for and reconciliation with the perpetrators of evil.

We see this prophetic method lived out from Moses to Malachi among the Hebrew prophets, in Jacob and Abinadi among the Nephites, as recounted in the Book of Mormon. We see this prophetic witness particularly clearly in the early ministry of Joseph Smith Jr. as he sought to give expression to radical justice for the poor in Zionic consecration of surplus. We see this prophetic witness in Thoreau, Gandhi, and Martin Luther King Jr., who all modeled that it is as important to not cooperate with evil as it is to cooperate with the good. We are privileged today to see courageous prophetic ministry in Ed Guy in Guatemala, Rupa Kumar in India, and Kathy Bachman in her work with Amnesty International. However, not just a few people are called to be prophetic; *all* of us are called. If all are called to be prophetic, what might be an agenda for a prophetic people to consider today?

What Is a Possible Agenda for a Prophetic People Today?

The monotheism of the prophets has universal implications. God is creator of all. All are made in God's image. Joseph Smith Jr. prophetically affirmed the worth of persons both in terms of creation and in Christ's redemption as follows:

One being is as precious in [God's] sight as the other. —Jacob 2:27

> Remember the worth of souls is great in the sight of God; for, behold, the Lord your Redeemer suffered death in the flesh; wherefore [God] suffered the pain of all....that all....might repent and come unto [God].
> —Doctrine and Covenants 16:3c

Thus all are of equal worth—there are no exceptions. Yet we are social creatures who need each other. We cannot live alone. The worth of persons has to be achieved socially. Technology has made the whole world a neighborhood. How do we make our planet a global Zionic family of equal brothers and sisters? What might be an agenda for a prophetic people to address? I suggest the following[2]:

1. *Addressing Xenophobia (Fear of Strangers)*

We live in a world imprisoned by nationalisms and ethnocentricities and thus we fear those who are different, the stranger. Hobsbawn, an authority on nationalism, states that "Xenophobia has become the most widespread mass ideology in the world."[3]

Jesus, however, knew no strangers. As an international church made up of many nations, peoples, and cultures, neither should we. In one form or other the following commandment is repeated thirty-six times in the Hebrew Bible:

> The alien who resides with you shall be to you as the citizen among you; you shall love the alien as yourself, for you were aliens in the land of Egypt: I am the Lord your God.—Leviticus 19:34 NRSV

In the parable of the final judgment, Jesus said: "I was a stranger and you welcomed me" (Matthew 25:35). I suggest we should be in the forefront of welcoming the one who is different, including immigrants, legal or illegal. Wherever God has created, humans have a right to be. International borders are human boundaries, not God's. We should also stand in our neighborhoods and communities with vulnerable minorities. In our early history we also knew what it was to be a vulnerable minority. "Stranger danger" is the prelude ultimately to genocide.

2. *Creating a Culture of Nonviolence and Respect for the Worth of All Persons.*

About 110 million people died in wars during the twentieth century. In the 1990s more than 90 percent of the casualties were civilians.[4] Today it is the most vulnerable who suffer from violence: women, children, and the elderly. You shall not kill! (Exodus 20:13), one of the Ten Commandments, is intensified in Jesus' teachings on the Sermon on the Mount:

> You have heard that it was said to those of ancient times "You shall not murder"; and "whoever murders shall be liable to judgment." But I say to you that if you are angry with a brother or sister, you will be liable to judgment; and if you insult a brother or sister, you will be liable to the council; and if you say, "You fool," you will be liable to the hell of fire.
> —Matthew 5:21–22 NRSV

> You have heard that it was said, "An eye for an eye and a tooth for a tooth." But I say to you, Do not resist an evildoer. But if anyone strikes you on the right cheek, turn the other also; and if anyone wants to sue you and take your coat, give your cloak as well; and if anyone forces you to go one mile, go also the second mile.
> You have heard that it was said, "You shall love your neighbor and hate your enemy." But I say to you, Love your enemies and pray for those who persecute you, so that you may be children of your Father in heaven; for he makes his sun rise on the evil and on the good, and sends rain on the righteous and on the unrighteous. For if you love those who love you, what reward do you have? Do not even the tax collectors do the same? And if you greet only your brothers and sisters, what more are you doing than others? Do not even the Gentiles do the same? Be perfect, therefore, as your heavenly Father is perfect.
> —Matthew 5:38–41, 43–48 NRSV

If there are no exceptions to the equal worth of all persons, we should not kill our enemies. When at his arrest Jesus disarmed Peter, Jesus disarmed every disciple after Peter. By accepting the cross rather than retaliating with the sword Jesus breaks the spiral of violence in himself. After the first 300 years of nonviolence, Christians progressively engaged in war. Christian history suggests that we ironically have become one of the most violent of world religions. Yet we, who are called to pursue peace, are to lead the world in beating swords into plow-shares and pioneering nonviolent methods of conflict resolution. The equal worth of all persons should also lead us to question capital punishment, torture, and inhumane prison conditions. If not, the crucifixion of Jesus and every Communion Sunday should help us reconsider.

3. *Being Accountable to the Poor and Oppressed*

It is important to glimpse the huge differences between rich and poor within our nations and between nations. If we turn away from these disturbing facts, then we do not know Jesus. Consider the following:

- About 12 million children die every year from entirely preventable disease and malnutrition.[5] In the last ten years this is about 120 million children--more than all the victims of war in the twentieth century. Poverty is the worst form of violence.

- No matter how poverty is measured, the gulf between the poor and rich in the world is becoming wider; the Southern and Northern Hemispheres are becoming polarized into two very different worlds.

  The poorest 20% of the world's people saw their share of global income decline from 2.3 percent to 1.4 percent in the past thirty years. Meanwhile the share of the richest twenty percent rose from seventy to eighty-five percent. That doubled the ratio of the shares of the richest and the poorest—from 30:1 to 61:1. In terms of net transfer of wealth from poor countries to rich countries about $43 billion a year flows from the Two-Thirds World to the First World.[6]

- In the country in which I presently live, the United States of America, the gap between rich and poor is also widening:

  Since the 1970s, the top 1 percent of households have doubled their share of the national wealth at the expense of everyone else....The top 1 percent of households has more wealth than the entire bottom 95 percent.[7]

In our financial stewardship we pursue peace when we pursue justice for the poor. Justice for the poor in our scriptures means redistribution of wealth. In Restoration scriptures our vision is inspired by "all things in common" (see Acts 2:44–45 and IV Nephi 1:4) with no poor among them (Doctrine and Covenants 36:2h–i).

4. *Commiting to a Life of Truthfulness*

"The truth," said Jesus, "shall make you free." However, the first casualty in war is frequently the truth. Most advertising is deceiving, whether it is for cigarettes, alcohol, or clothes. Governments frequently lie by propaganda or "misinformation." One can go on. Jesus is clear though: "Let your word be 'Yes, Yes' or 'No, No'; anything more than this comes from the evil one" (Matthew 5:37). We are called to reveal and speak the truth, not only of the gospel but of poverty, oppression, and violence.

5. *Developing a Culture of Equal Rights and Partnership between Men and Women*

There are deep roots in our religious tradition about equal rights and partnership between men and women. It is how creation began:

> So God created humankind in his image, in the image of God he created them; male and female he created them.—Genesis 1:27 NRSV

In the ministry of Jesus we see women raised up from their oppression, talked with as equals, encouraged to study, and being followers with Jesus' traveling band of disciples. Women were there at the foot of the cross. Women were at the burial. Women were the first witnesses of the resurrection. Paul grasped the implications of baptism into Christ as follows:

> As many of you as were baptized into Christ have clothed yourselves with Christ. There is no longer Jew or Greek, there is no longer slave or free, there is no longer male and female; for all of you are one in Christ Jesus.—Galatians 3:27–28 NRSV

In the early Restoration movement a statement included in the Doctrine and Covenants in 1835 talks of marriage as partnership in the following terms: "You both mutually agree to be each other's companion, husband and wife..." (Doctrine and Covenants 111:2b).

The early Reorganization's rejection of polygamy was an affirmation of the worth of women. The recent ordination of women continues that tradition in the Reorganization of affirming the equal giftedness and calling of women.

We live in a world, though, where women do not enjoy equality. And in our religious movement we do not always treat women as equals. Half of the women in North America will be abused at some time in their life. According to a United Nations report in the 1970s, "Women constitute half the world's population, perform nearly two thirds of its work hours, receive one tenth of the world's income and own less than one hundredth of the world's property." Female circumcision and female infanticide still happens in some parts of the globe. Dowry systems cause oppression. Women still come second in many countries in terms of educational opportunities, employment opportunities, and legal rights.

We still have some way to go in terms of fully developing a culture of equal rights and partnership between men and women. We are called to be in the forefront.

6. *Respecting the Environment*

The Genesis story of a good creation places humans in the role of caretakers. Jewish scriptures reflect a continuing concern for the environment. We are also called to render an account of this part of our stewardship:

> Although it is true that the growing populations in the Two-Thirds World stress the ecosystem, we in the [One-Third World—North America, Europe, Australasia] must realize that most of the planet's problems are caused by the production and consumption of the [One-Third World]. "The industrialized countries of the [One-Third World] are home to one-fifth of the world's population, yet they consume two-thirds of the world's food, three-quarters of its energy and minerals and 85 percent of its wood." The United States alone, with less than 5 percent of the world's population, consumes about 60 percent of the world's natural gas, 40 percent of coal and aluminum, and 30 percent of nickel, copper, and petroleum. The United States accounts for a quarter of the global energy consumption and produces a quarter of the world's air pollution.[8]

The dangers posed by human carelessness to the fragile eco-systems of planet Earth remind us of this dimension of being a prophetic people:

> These are portentous times. The lives of many are being sacrificed unnecessarily to the gods of war, greed, and avarice. The land is being desecrated by the thoughtless waste of vital resources. You must obey my commandments and be in the forefront of those who would mediate this needless destruction while there is yet day.—Doctrine and Covenants 150:7

Conclusion

There are two kinds of prophets: true prophets and false prophets. False prophets speak peace when there is no peace. They hide the injustices and oppression of the status quo, protect the rich and the powerful, and sanctify the present culture, using religion to do so. They tame the radical demands of the gospel and ignore the poor. The true prophet speaks the truth fearlessly and confronts the culture with the living word of God. All humans are of equal worth—despise none, exploit none. The rich are accountable.

There is a cost to this prophetic confrontation with our own culture. It is a way that requires courage. At the very best prophets are often without honor in their own country and in their own culture. More seriously, prophets are stoned, burned to death, shot, beheaded, or crucified. Cultures can often cruelly reject those who bring a judgment that threatens the powerful and questions the privileged, that reveals the truth. Yet even reluctant prophets like Jonah can bring a whole city to repentance, and the blood of prophetic martyrs can sow the seeds of cultural transformation.

After crucifixion there is the hope of resurrection. After resurrection there is the promise of Pentecost, Holy Spirit, endowment. When God's Spirit triumphs completely, when the equal worth of persons and respect for all of life finds expression in our use of the environment, economics, family life, education, workplaces, neighborhoods, and in the way we resolve conflict, then is Zion come, then is *shalom* realized. Until then, the kingdom is still at hand, at the door, beckoning and calling, pregnant with new possibilities—new wine for new wineskins, a new spirit for new cultural expressions. With a global vision, fostered by our international church, we are called to act personally in our congregations. The transformation of our congregational culture is the first step to transforming the world.

For Reflection and Discussion

1. Look back at each of the chapters and summarize what the author has said that gives us insight into peace through the teachings of Jesus Christ.

2. What do you see differently about your own culture as a result of this study?

3. Create as many endings to the following sentence as you can that reflect how we can live out our prophetic role. "Because we believe in the worth of persons we will...."

4. Give examples of how you have seen the prophetic method from the biblical tradition lived out.

5. Discuss each one of the six agenda items for a prophetic people. List the examples and items discussed by each of the authors under one of the six agenda items for a prophetic people. Make the list under two headings: "Accomplishments" and "Challenges."

6. List some concrete suggestions for actions you (individually or as a group) can take for each of the six agenda items.

7. How will the gospel of Jesus Christ be played out in our work as prophets of peace?

Notes

1. See Dennis C. Duling and Norman Perrin, *The New Testament: Proclamation and Parenesis, Myth and History* (Fort Worth, Texas: Harcourt Brace College Publishing, 1994), chapter 3.
2. I am grateful for Hans Küng's work on a global ethic, which contributed to my thinking. See Hans Küng and Karl-Josef Kuschel, eds., *A Global Ethic—The Declaration of the Parliament of the World's Religions* (London: SCM Press,1993).
3. E. J. Hobsbawn, *Nations and Nationalism Since 1780—Programme, Myth, Reality* (Cambridge: Cambridge University Press,1992), 170.
4. Ruth Leger Sivard, *World Military and Social Expenditures 1996* (Washington, D.C.: World Priorities), 5, 19; and Carol Bellamy, *The State of the World's Children 1996* (New York: UNICEF/Oxford University Press), 13.
5. Bellamy, 1998, 6.
6. J. Milburn Thompson, *Justice and Peace—A Christian Primer* (Maryknoll, New York: Orbis, 1997), 35, 42.
7. Chuck Collins, Betsy Leondar-Wright, and Holly Sklar, *Shifting Fortunes: The Perils of the Growing American Wealth Gap* (Boston: United for a Fair Economy, 1999), 5.
8. Thompson, 66.

Contributors

Howard S. Sheehy Jr. was a full-time minister of the Reorganized Church of Jesus Christ of Latter Day Saints for forty years, from 1960 until his retirement in 2000. After eight years as a field appointee he was ordained a member of the Council of Twelve Apostles, ministering in North America, the South Pacific, and in the Orient for ten years. He then served as a member of the Quorum of the First Presidency, until his retirement. He and his wife, Florine, have three children (John, Lisa, and Michael) and seven grandchildren.

Rick Sarre is associate professor at the University of South Australia School of International Business. He is a member of the World Church Peace Committee and an adjunct professor at Graceland College. He and his wife, Debra, live in Adelaide, South Australia, with their children, Millicent and Elliott.

Etienne P. Faana is a native of Rairoa, French Polynesia. He has lived and studied in France, the United States, French Polynesia, and Fiji, earning degrees in French, liberal arts, and religion with additional studies in history, social studies, and law. As a full-time minister since 1966, Etienne has ministered in the Haiti and Caribbean regions and in French Polynesia. With his wife, Jeannine, they have raised four children (Moeata Marie-Laure, Terai Jane, Moana Stevens, and Valimiti Gwendoline) and enjoy four grandchildren.

Barbara (McFarlane) Higdon holds a Ph.D. from the University of Missouri–Columbia and an honorary Doctor of Humane

Letters from Graceland College. She taught English and speech at Texas Southern and Graceland, was vice president for academic affairs and dean of faculty at Park College, and president of Graceland College. Since her retirement she has worked as a volunteer mediator and trainer in the Dispute Resolution Program at Lifeline in Vista, California. Currently she is provost of the Lamoni campus of Graceland University. She is the author of two books: *Good News for Today* and *Committed to Peace.*

Kerstin Jeske Kristiansen and Eva Erickson were both born and raised in East Germany. Kerstin grew up in the RLDS Church as the daughter of the national church leader, whereas Eva grew up Protestant and did not join the RLDS Church until she was twenty. They both left Germany for the United States in 1991 (two years after the wall came down) to study at Graceland College. Kerstin is presently living in Norway and is a field minister working as an assistant region administrator and Quorum of Seventy president, with responsibilities for Scandinavia, Netherlands, Belgium, France, and Spain. Eva lives in Independence, Missouri, with her husband, John, and young daughter, Miriam.

Joseph Sunday Charlie is a Transformation 2000 church planter in Lagos, Nigeria, where he lives with his wife, Affiong Charlie, and their daughter, Emma. He is a native of Abak, Akwa Ibom State, Nigeria, where he earned a national diploma in management. He then attended Park College where he completed a bachelor's degree in management and a masters degree in public administration. In addition to English, Joseph has a working knowledge of French and Swahili.

Mary Ooko was born on Christmas Day in Kisumu, Kenya. She is now a Transformation 2000 church planter living in Johannesburg, South Africa, with her husband and four daughters. Before this assignment Mary taught in a primary school and later trained teachers for deaf children at the Kenya Institute of Special Education. Mary acquired her early education in Kenya. Later she studied at the State University of New York, the College at New Paltz, obtaining a bachelor's degree in speech and hearing. Mary also earned a master's degree in religious studies from Park College.

Bunda C. Chibwe [Chichi] was born at Lubunda, Mwense, in Luapula Province, Zambia. He is a convert to the RLDS Church and has served the church since 1982 as local pastor, national treasurer, national president, associate region administrator, Quorum of Seventy president, and since World Conference 2000 as a member of the Council of Twelve Apostles with assignment to cross-cultural ministries and Africa. He holds a master of arts in religion degree from Park College. Bunda and his wife, Jenny, have four children (Cecilia, Andrew, Manasseh and Deborah).

Rupavathy Kumar was born in the city of Madurai in the southern state of Tamil Nadu, India. She has earned three bachelor's degrees and two master's degrees (in Tamil literature and social work) and has distinguished herself by establishing one of the first shelters for abused women and children in India and an educational street theater company. She was honored by the 1996 World Conference, which presented her with the International Human Rights Award for Service to Humanity. Rupa's family includes her husband, Sam, and two children, Cordelia and Daniel.

Hiroshi Yamada is a native of Nagasaki, Japan. He graduated with a degree in economics from Chuo University in Tokyo. He also attended Graceland College in Lamoni, Iowa, and studied religion at the School of the Restoration. Serving the church as a full-time minister since 1963, his assignments have included presiding elder, missionary elder, administrator of Seijo Nursery and English Language School, assistant to the Asia Field apostle, treasurer of the Orient and Asia Field, Temple School, and the Peace and Justice team. He has written a history of the church in Japan. In 2000 Hiroshi and his wife, Mizuko, retired to Japan to be with their children (Yasuhiro and Kaoru) and their grandchildren (Kugo and Namio).

Andrew Bolton is the Peace and Justice coordinator for the World Church. He is a native of Preston, Lancashire, England. He holds a master of arts in religion degree from Park College and a Ph.D. from the University of Wales. He taught English as a Second Language at the Seijo English Academy in Tokyo, was a research assistant at the University of Wales, gardener in Tangstedt, Schleswig-Holstein, West Germany, and worked in education in England, most recently as Religious Education/ Multicultural/Citizenship advisor for the Leicester City Council. Andrew and his wife, Jewell Holmes, have two sons, Matthew and David.